WATER GARDENS

SUNSET BOOKS

President and VP Sales: Richard A. Smeby
VP, Editorial Director: Bob Doyle
Production Director: Lory Day
Art Director. Vasken Guiragossian

Water Gardens was produced in conjunction with

ST. REMY MULTIMEDIA

President/Chief Executive Officer: Fernand Lecoq
President/Chief Operating Officer: Pierre Léveillé
Vice President, Finance: Natalie Watanabe
Managing Editor: Carolyn Jackson
Managing Art Director: Diane Denoncourt
Production Manager: Michelle Turbide
Marketing Manager: Christopher Jackson

Staff for this Book:

Senior Editors: Jim McRae, Pierre Home-Douglas
Art Director: Odette Sévigny
Assistant Editors: Rob Lutes, Jennifer Ormston
Researcher: Adam Van Sertima
Designer: Sara Grynspan
Picture Editor: Jennifer Meltzer
Contributing Illustrators: Gilles Beauchemin, Michel Blais,
    Jean-Guy Doiron, Jacques Perrault, La Bande Créative
Production Coordinator: Dominique Gagné
System Coordinator: Eric Beaulieu
Scanner Operator: Martin Francoeur
Technical Support: Jean Sirois
Proofreader: Judy Yelon
Indexer: Linda Cardella Cournoyer

Book Consultants:

Don Vandervort
David Nanasi
Virginia Hayes

Cover:

Design: Robin Weiss
Photography: Saxon Holt

Landscape:

Chris Jacobsen, Garden Art,
San Francisco

5 6 7 8 9 0 QPD/QPD 9 8 7 6 5 4 3 2 1 0

Copyright © 1997
Published by Sunset Publishing Corp., Menlo Park, CA 94025.
First edition. All rights reserved, including the right of
    reproduction in whole or in part in any form.

ISBN 0-376-03848-9
Library of Congress Catalog Card Number: 97-60080
Printed in the United States

For additional copies of *Water Gardens* or any other Sunset
book, call 1-800-643-8030, ext. 544, or see our
website at: www.sunsetbooks.com

WATER GARDENS

Sunset

Table of Contents

The World of
WATER
GARDENS

Whether it takes the form of a simple stone fountain bubbling peacefully in the corner of a patio or a full-fledged natural pond, stocked with colorful koi carp and a plethora of plants, a water garden is a dramatic addition to any space—indoors or out. For thousands of years, the shimmer and sound of water, along with its essential role in sustaining life, have endowed this element with great religious and mystical significance. Virtually every culture and every age has adopted the practice of gardening with water, altering and refining it to suit their own particular philosophies and practical needs. The following brief history of water gardens will provide you with inspiration and historical background you can call upon when it comes time to create your own restful world of water.

Over the centuries, water gardening traditions have been continually shared between cultures. With its formal shape, classical statues, and colonnaded building, the elegant water garden at Studley Royal in England reveals both French and Italian influences.

An Ancient Tradition

Mankind's fascination with water gardens is almost as old as civilization itself. Necessity may have been the mother of their invention, some 3,000 years before Christ on the scorched, desert plains of Mesopotamia and Egypt. The civilizations here were situated beside very fertile rivers—Mesopotamia between the Tigris and Euphrates in what is now Iraq, and Egypt on the banks of the life-giving Nile. Survival for both societies depended on the ability to channel water from these rivers to transform the barren landscape into arable land. Irrigation canals and ponds were constructed to water the crops.

But as fish, lotuses, and other plants were added to beautify these simple channels, the practical function of water was broadened to include an important spiritual one—paying reverence to its pow-

This placid pool—part of the mosque at Isfahan in today's Iran—recalls the calm of the *pairi-daeza*, the ancient paradise garden of the Persians.

The garden at Hasht Behesht (the eight paradises) in Iran contains one major design variation from the traditional *chahar bagh*: The pool of life at the center was replaced by a pavilion, here reflected in one of the garden's water channels.

er to give life. The water garden, lush with foliage in the midst of the parched, desert environment, came to stand as a powerful symbol of paradise, and of life itself.

With the rise and fall of subsequent empires and the inexorable migration of populations, the practice of water gardening spread slowly throughout the ancient world. Water gardens became regular features in inner courtyards, providing weary travelers with a cool, peaceful place to rest before continuing their journeys. In some cases, water from the garden was channeled to small canals under homes to cool the air inside.

In the most elaborate examples, ancient water gardening reached the pinnacle of artistic expression. The most famous water garden in history, the fabled Hanging Gardens of Babylon, was constructed in 600 B.C. Its stunning terraces, streams, and stone balconies earned it a place as one of the Seven Wonders of the Ancient World.

The sole remaining example of this earliest generation of water gardens—albeit one now in ruins—lies at Pasargardae, near Isfahan in what is today Iran. Planted per-

sonally by the founder of the Persian Empire, Cyrus the Great, in 546 B.C., it is a walled rectangular garden, bordered by two pavilions and two palaces. In old Persian, it was called *pairidaeza*, the root for the English word "paradise."

Sometime after the Pasargardae garden was constructed, the Persians began to develop and incorporate another design into the *pairidaeza*. The *chahar bagh*, or "fourfold" garden, was a walled square divided into four equal parts by two canals. A "pool of life" was located at the center. Each section was planted with fruit and shade trees and various flowers and was irrigated by small channels.

The Persian design showed remarkable resilience through the centuries, surviving Persia's fall to Macedonia under Alexander the Great in the 4th century B.C., outlasting the successful Roman invasion 300 years later, and enduring through invasion by the Muslim Arabs in A.D. 642.

Indeed, because the *chahar bagh* mirrored descriptions of the paradise garden in Islam's holy book, the Koran, the Muslims embraced the design fully, and took it with them when they conquered Syria, India, Spain, North Africa, and Turkey. The Islamic garden, therefore, is the perfect place to begin a cultural tour of the water garden.

ISLAMIC WATER GARDENS

Not surprisingly, water was the dominating element in Islamic water gardens. For desert dwellers, not only was water a necessary element for survival, but it also was in short supply and had to be used sparingly. So, like the ancient Middle Eastern peoples before them, the Muslims adapted what was essentially an agricultural irrigation system to reflect their deep reverence for the life-sustaining liquid.

Canals were left uncovered, enabling everyone to enjoy the peaceful passage of water. Capitalizing on the reflection of surrounding buildings, wide but shallow pools appeared to be deep and other-worldly. Fountains often projected a single, delicate stream of water, providing a soothing sound

Constructed in the 14th century by Moorish king Yusef I, the exquisite water garden at the Court of the Myrtles in the Alhambra in Spain serves a practical as well as an esthetic purpose—the breeze across its water cools the palace.

The sunken, star-shaped pool at Amber Fort Palace in Rajastan, India, evokes the Islamic fourfold garden, or *chahar bagh*. It was built in the 16th century by Moghul rulers Man Singh I and Jai Singh I.

to passersby. The Muslims stuck closely to the *pairidaeza* and *chahar bagh* models *(page 9)* adopted from the Persians.

In Spain: When a group of North African Muslims called the Moors invaded Spain in A.D. 711, they brought with them their Islamic reverence for water and their practice of water gardening. Because Spain had a relatively rich water supply, the Moors were able to use the element more freely. The resulting courtyard gardens, while representative facets of Islam design, were far more exuberant than their predecessors. Today, the ancient Moorish Gardens at Alhambra *(opposite)* and Granada provide striking examples of this heightened vitality.

In India: Several centuries later, the Moghuls, descendants of the legendary Mongol leader Genghis Khan, carried the Islamic tradition across the Indus River into India. Throughout the 16th and 17th centuries, the Moghul rulers proved to be exceptional gardeners. Again, the friendlier climate and more plentiful water sources meant that water was used more freely, and often to higher effect. But the Hindustani people felt differently about water than did their Islamic conquerors. Their reverence was based on religion, not survival, and they were less inclined to the sharp, clean geometric shapes of the Muslims. Thus the Moghul garden evolved into another subtle variation of the Islamic—less spartan than the *chahar bagh*, and less constrained by a scarcity of water, but still influenced by its Islamic predecessors. Perhaps the most wondrous vestige of this period is the Taj Mahal in Agra.

ITALIAN WATER GARDENS

The earliest Italian water gardens contained a mix of Greek and Persian influences, but with the dawn of the Roman Empire, a singular style would emerge—and in true Roman fashion, it was a grand one. Baths, pools, canals, waterfalls, and fountains all featured prominently in the Roman garden. The most elaborate of these often featured classical buildings, statues, and towering colonnades.

The fall of the Roman Empire spelled the end of this tradition, but with the Italian Renaissance in the 15th century came a rebirth of artistic water gardening. Believing that beauty was to be found in the harmony of all parts, artists adapted ancient classical ideas to more imaginative forms in order to link home, garden, and the surrounding terrain into a unified whole. Fountains appeared in all sorts of new shapes. Many stunning examples of Baroque fountains still grace Rome's central piazzas.

Unity of home and garden is beautifully realized at Villa Carlotta in Italy's Lake Como region. The small pool, with its thriving ring of lilies, artistically frames the fountain, a central feature of Italian water gardens.

FRENCH WATER GARDENS

The water gardening tradition in France had its roots in the moats, fish ponds, and food gardens of Medieval Europe. As the country slowly emerged from the relative darkness of the Middle Ages, these functional features were transformed into pleasure gardens. The Italian Renaissance exerted an enormous influence. Classical statues and fountains found their way into the French garden, as did parterres—patterns formed by the careful arrangement of plants within a border. The classic French garden, with its highly formal, ornate, and controlled design, reflected the rise of rationalism in the 17th and 18th centuries and the belief that the forces of nature must be subsumed by the intellect.

The French inclination toward order in the garden is evident at Versailles *(left)*, Louis XIV's grand palace, located just outside Paris. Symmetrically shaped and meticulously maintained, the gardens stand as monuments to man's control over nature.

The Italian influence is manifest in the exquisite classical statues found in some of Versailles' pools *(below)*.

ENGLISH WATER GARDENS

Though the English created stunning formal gardens at various times in their history, it is their landscape ponds that have exerted the greatest influence. The tradition had its origin in the late 17th century, as a reaction to the ostentatious and formal gardens of the French. By that time, English writers such as Joseph Addison and Alexander Pope had begun to extol the virtues of the natural landscape in their poetry.

The change from formal to informal was gradual, and prominent designers developed specific variations, but the essence and central focus of an English water garden remained the water itself. Large, irregularly shaped ponds were set in natural surroundings to highlight the reflective properties of water. Over the following centuries, waterfalls and exotic plants, imported from the East, also came into favor, lending their own splendor to English natural gardens.

The dazzling colors of pondside blooms play off the placid surface of an English pond at Exbury.

The garden of Wang Shih Yuan, constructed during the late Ming Dynasty (1368-1644) illustrates the use of plantings and stone to create the appearance of a natural pond. Buildings surrounding the pond—a common feature in Chinese gardens—do not detract from its natural beauty.

CHINESE WATER GARDENS

By the time the English had succeeded in creating their natural ponds, the Chinese were already well-established masters of the art. Adherents of Taoist philosophy, based on the teachings of Lao-tzu, the Chinese held that the way to enlightened living was through communion with nature. Their water gardens, stunning artistic imitations of the natural world, were designed to aid this process by providing a place of peaceful contemplation where this crucial connection could be made. The garden was considered a microcosm of the world, which for the Chinese was divided into female and male elements—the Yin and the Yang—represented in the garden by water and mountains. Water was used in every way possible. Streams and waterfalls joined ponds and lakes in creating grand waterscapes. Rocks, earth, plants, and animals were added judiciously to represent other aspects of the natural world and complete a living portrait of nature. The connections were not always literal. A few stones in a stream, for example, could represent islands in a vast ocean; a few rocks strategically placed, a mountain range.

Meditative Gardens

A sense of serenity pervades this Japanese stroll garden *(left)*. The pond's reflective qualities are highlighted by brilliant summer blooms mirrored on its surface.

The Japanese water basin, or *tsukubai (below)*, allows guests to wash their mouths and hands before taking tea. Even when not used for its original purpose, its gentle trickle produces a feeling of tranquillity.

As the modern world becomes increasingly stressful, more and more people are searching for a sanctuary—a peaceful oasis for relaxation where daily concerns are soothed away and restful contemplation is given a chance to revitalize the soul. A meditative garden, filled with calming sights and sounds, neatly fills that need.

Meditative gardens can take any number of forms, from the exaggerated control exhibited in French gardens to the more natural beauty of English-style ponds. The type you choose depends on what you feel promotes the greatest degree of serenity and pleasure.

No matter which style of garden you choose, its features can probably be traced to the Japanese tradition. Designed specifically to promote the quiet study of nature, the Japanese garden will, at the very least, offer some inspirational fodder for creating your own meditative garden.

Religious roots: The Japanese water garden arose out of the Shinto religious belief that gods were spirits of nature. Shintoism espouses a religious reverence for the natural world, and the spiritual need to commune with it. In every Japanese garden, therefore, the goal is to create the impression of nature, and the water garden provided one means of making that vital connection.

To imitate nature, particularly in smaller gardens where space prohibits an honest reproduction of a natural landscape, the Japanese use simplification—the reduction of some aspect of the natural world to its essential quality. The gardener uses specially chosen items and symbols to *imply* nature as a whole. Carefully placed rocks are evocative of mountains, for example, and water, even in the smallest basin, can create the impression of a much larger pond.

The notion of simplification also reflects the Japanese view of the person as participant—not just as observer—in the garden. In capturing only the essence of a particular landscape, visitors are invited to provide the missing detail by using their imaginations. When the mind is activated in this way, the garden has succeeded in precipitating a deep contemplation of the natural world.

Water: It is not hard to understand the importance of water in the gardens of Japan—an island nation crisscrossed by rivers and dotted with lush lakes. Waterfalls, streams, and ponds are used to evoke this natural world. Where water is not desirable or feasible, subtle methods are often used to create its impression. A stunning example of this is found in the dry landscape gardens that were first created by Zen Buddhist monks in the late 6th century. Here, water is represented by gravel or sand, islands by stones. Each day the sand or gravel is raked, and each day, wind and rain erase all traces of that raking. In this way, the gravel conveys the constantly changing form of water in a pond.

The passage of time: Japanese gardeners are also adept in their use of light to convey the passage of time —an integral part of nature.

Flowers, trees, mossy rocks, and other elements are positioned to receive light at different times of the day. Even shadows are considered in the orchestrated plan. The garden is also designed to herald seasonal change. While many gardens in Japan are planted to display intense flashes of color in summer, just as many feature early bloomers to highlight the joyful renewal of spring. Relatively neutral background plantings allow these seasonal features to assume prominence in the overall design.

The Japanese dry garden is a paragon of architectural impressionism. Here, two carefully selected stones stranded in the center of a bed of gravel conjure up the image of islands in a vast sea. The gravel is raked to suggest the rippled surface of water.

Enclosure: Another important element in the Japanese garden, and one particularly relevant for any meditative garden, is enclosure—setting the garden apart from the outside world. Plantings, walls, and fences, often up to 7 feet tall, help provide privacy around the garden, while trees, such as leafy Japanese maples, for instance, can be used to provide overhead cover, if that is desired. In areas that cannot be enclosed, the concept of borrowed scenery comes into play. Here, the landscape surrounding the garden is not shut out, but rather is incorporated into, or made a backdrop for, the garden design.

Stones and plants: Stone, in the form of bridges, basins, lanterns, and other accents, plays a vital role in the Japanese garden. Placed in groups, stones can be used to create various formations. As with all other elements in the Japanese garden, stone features must appear perfectly natural. Plants are effec-

Stone lanterns, such as the one shown above, are a common feature of Japanese gardens. Typically weathered, or even cracked, they provide a subtle contrast with the natural features of the garden.

The handsome stones lining the banks of this Japanese stream *(right)* have been carefully placed to look as if the forces of nature settled them there ages ago.

tive so long as they too appear to grow naturally. Again, this means carefully planned placement that should look random. Groupings of three plants, rather than two, which create a nonuniform shape are most effective. Scale is also crucial, particularly in a small garden. No plant should look too large or small.

Your meditative water garden: Knowledge of these and other principles of Japanese water gardening will give you the basis for creating a meditative haven of your own, but by no means must you stick religiously to them. The Japanese tradition evolved, in part, as a response to the landscape of the country. Look at the natural world around your own home for inspiration when designing and choosing the elements of your garden. However, since the garden is meant to be *your* personal sanctuary, the final arbiter should always be your own taste and preferences. Then it will offer you a pleasurable retreat.

Water Features
IN YOUR YARD

*Quiet reflecting pools, dancing waterfalls,
and gurgling streams—water in all its many forms
brings both energy and charm into a garden. Whether
it reflects the sky and clouds, a piece of garden sculpture,
or the arching branches of a tree, a garden pool creates
an ever-changing picture. The cooling effect of a fountain
or waterfall on hot summer days and evenings is as
welcome now as in times past. And goldfish or koi
dimpling the surface of a fish pond continue to captivate.
For gardeners, a water garden opens up a whole new
world of possibilities. In this chapter, we'll show you
the options for water features in your own yard and
help you decide which will be best for you.*

This tranquil, naturalistic pool looks as though it has always
been here. Boulders and trailing plants by the water's edge
hide the pond's building materials, and potted plants unify
the various areas of the garden.

Garden Pools

Even if you don't have the time, space, or money necessary to build an elaborate pool, it doesn't mean that water has no place in your garden. Almost all of today's home owners can choose to build pools that will complement their gardens in both size and style.

If your space is very limited, or if you want a pond simply to bring interest to a corner of the garden, a patio, or sitting area, you can opt for a small accent pool or even a tub garden *(page 28)*.

Generally speaking, garden pools are either formal or informal in style, although of course, there are ways of blending the two styles.

FORMAL POOLS

On the spacious estate gardens of England in years past, a garden pool was frequently a generous circle, oval, or rectangle—slightly

The long lines of this formal pool draw the eye to the relaxing seat at the opposite end. Even rows of potted plants reflect the symmetry that is typical of formal designs and provide an interesting variation in height.

FORMAL POOL SHAPES
Formal pools are characterized by clean, geometric lines—whether straight or curved—and neat, regular borders.

raised—set in the center of an area and surrounded by spacious walks. This meant it could be viewed from every side. Nowadays, there are still a few gardens large enough to accommodate such pools, but in most cases the pool must be set near some border if there is to be enough room for anything else.

To evoke the old style in a modern garden, choose a formal pool. Generally, a formal pool looks as though it has been added to the landscape, rather than appearing there naturally. It has regular, clean lines, and carefully selected—often tailored-looking—plantings.

Formal pools have simple geometric shapes: hexagons, circles, ovals, squares, or L-shapes. Size is not important; the pool can be scaled up or down to fit the available space and harmonize with the surroundings. The edging material is usually regularly sized and evenly spaced: brick, flagstone, or tile are the most common choices. Fountains and sculpture are characteristic accessories.

Traditionally, a formal pool would have been made of concrete or clay, but today there are other materials that are more easily

RAISED POOLS

A raised pool is an interesting design option for a variety of reasons: It is one way to add varying height to a relatively flat garden landscape; it brings the water garden closer to the eye level of a seated person; it is safer when young children are around; if surrounded by a wall with a wide coping, it offers a pleasant seat from which to observe the garden; and it makes pond maintenance easier because bending and stooping are reduced. Furthermore, since a fully raised pool only requires excavation for the wall footings, it can be a good choice in a yard whose very rocky soil is hard to work.

One disadvantage of raised pools is that water temperature fluctuates more rapidly than it does in sunken pools, causing problems for fish. With some designs, you can counteract this by adding insulation within the pond wall.

You can build a raised pool from the same materials used for sunken pools. See pages 138-143 for information on building raised pools.

Colorful glazed ceramic tiles lend an old-world flair to this lushly planted raised pool in the formal style. Clumps of tall green plants add interest because of their height and provide a contrast to the patchwork colors of the tiles.

installed by the do-it-yourselfer, preformed fiberglass or flexible liners, for example, that produce excellent results. For more information, see page 56 for a discussion of the various pool materials.

Formal pools can be raised above ground level, semiraised, or sunken, depending on the site and the border effect you wish. A raised pool may take more effort and materials because of the wall that must be constructed around the pool, but it provides surfaces for sitting and sunning, as well as for container plants and decorations.

INFORMAL POOLS

An informal pool is almost any body of water without square corners, perpendicular walls, or artificial edges in sight. It should look like it was designed by nature itself.

The variety of choices open to the designer is as wide-ranging as the designs are beautiful. Yours could be modeled after an alpine pool, a tiny spring at some desert oasis, or a water retreat that caught your eye on your last vacation.

Oriental gardens are an excellent source of inspiration for natural-looking ponds, although they often require a great deal of general maintenance. Or you can choose to install a pond that looks like it exists naturally on your property. Use native stone and soil around it, and include plants common to the area in which you live.

The edges of the pool are usually camouflaged with lush plantings,

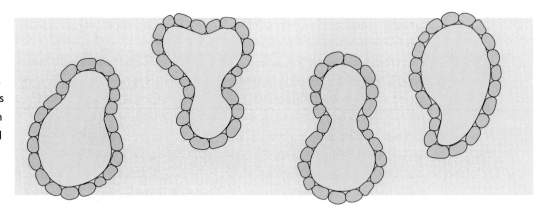

INFORMAL POOL SHAPES

Any shape that's curved or rounded, without sharp edges or straight lines, can work as an informal pool. Simple shapes tend to look most natural.

AN INFORMAL POOL IN A FORMAL GARDEN

If you have an established garden in a formal style, but would prefer an informal pool, try constructing a more formal, geometric border around the pool. Fill in the space with plantings and loose materials such as pebbles or wood chips.

Unevenly spaced border stones and the variety of plants growing right up to the water's edge help give this pool its informal character. The small stones offer a contrast in textures.

A water feature inside your house offers all the advantages of an outdoor garden, year-round. The formal shape of this indoor pool is offset by the pleasing roughness and irregular shapes of the rocks that form the edging. Rocks used inside the pool must be smooth so they won't injure the koi.
Landscape contractor: John Nishizawa, Co., Inc.

rocks, soil, and other materials. A bog garden of plants that prefer very moist soil, or even standing water, can be planted in the shallows of the pond or at the edge; a pebble beach can make an attractive natural-looking edging for one side of the pond. For more on borders and edgings, see page 61.

Most older natural pools feature shells that are constructed of hand-packed reinforced concrete; today, a more common choice for do-it-yourselfers, and one that's easier to install, is a pool liner or pre-formed fiberglass shell.

An informal pool is enjoyable to create, but it is also demanding. In many ways, the actual construction process could prove to be less difficult than deciding on the way to artfully blend your chosen materials and plantings.

Informal designs seem to fit comfortably in limited space. However, a boulder-framed pool requires ample elbow room. Boulders fill up space quickly, so the shell of the pool itself has to be sizable in order to remain in scale.

If you are going to do it yourself, the only rule is this: Keep it simple. Complex designs are difficult to manage during construction and often don't achieve the desired effect. Also, if the design has very contoured edges, water may not circulate freely because it might become trapped in the pockets and small pools.

A Living Pond

Plants and fish add an extra element of interest to a garden pond. But to make sure your pool meets their needs, you'll have to make certain decisions before you even start.

Planning for plants: Most plants require at least four hours of sunlight daily. In addition, different water plants need different depths of water. Ledges or shelves about 10 inches wide can be built around the edges of the pond, at varying depths (about 10 inches and about 18 inches below the water line are the most common choices).

Plants generally do not grow very well in moving water, so keep them away from a waterfall or fountain. And keep in mind that water plants vary in their hardiness, so you'll need to select those that are appropriate for your climate. Turn to Chapter 4 for more about plants and their needs.

Planning for fish: Pond fish require clean water with lots of oxygen. Depending on the type and number of fish you have, you may require a pump or a filter, or both. See page 59 for more information.

Fish don't adapt well to rapid fluctuations in water temperature, so sunken pools, which tend to have more stable water temperature than raised pools, may be a better choice—although it is possible to insulate a raised pool. Pond depth is also important: Water temperature tends to fluctuate more in shallow pools. Protection from cold winds is also a good idea.

Varying the depth of the pond will offer the fish a variety of water temperatures at any one time. (Shallow water will warm up more quickly.) Deeper water offers refuge from predators such as raccoons or cats. The minimum depth for a

Water plants offer a new gardening experience. Some grow in submerged pots, while others, such as the purple-flowered water hyacinth (*Eichhornia*) shown at left, float free on the water.

fish pond is about 18 inches. Larger fish, such as koi, which can grow to about 2½ feet long, need larger and deeper ponds. In colder climates, fish can be kept outdoors over the winter provided the pond doesn't freeze solid. Depths of about 2½ feet and a pump to keep the water constantly circulating should suffice.

Keep in mind that in many places, ponds over two feet in depth are subject to the same safety regulations as swimming pools, and may require fencing and other precautions. Check with your local building department.

Full sun is not desirable for fish. Floating plants and floating-leafed plants do provide shade. However, many koi keepers avoid plants, both to show off the fish better, and because koi have a habit of uprooting plants. You can make a separate area for plants, with a barrier to keep the koi out. Or try covering the soil with a layer of clean gravel. Bridges and other structures can also provide shade. See Chapter 5 for more information on fish.

A BALANCED ECOSYSTEM

Fish are the visual showstoppers of most garden ponds. But they can also serve a more practical purpose by helping to create a proper ecological balance in their watery environment.

Garden pools are often plagued by excessive algae growth, which makes the water look green. Fish help with the algae problem because they feed on it. As an added bonus, they also devour insect larvae, helping to minimize the mosquito problem around your pool.

Plants, too, play their role. First, because algae thrive on sunlight, a key step is to deprive them of it. Plants that cover some of the surface of the water will compete with the algae for the available light. Oxygenating plants, such as anacharis, take up carbon dioxide and release oxygen for the use of other plants and fish.

Water snails also feed on algae, but when they die, the snails release toxic ammonia into the pond. If your filter system is inadequate, this may be a problem.

To strike a good balance in a 6- by 8-foot pond, try two 3- to 5-inch fish, six water snails, and two bunches of oxygenating grasses (six stems to a bunch). Ideally, plants should cover about 60 percent of the surface of the water.

Even if your garden pond isn't primarily a fish pond, a few fish can help keep algae under control. But don't feed fish too much—excess nutrients from uneaten food encourage the growth of algae.

Tub Gardens

A water feature doesn't have to be large to be interesting. In fact, water elements on a smaller scale bring many of the same pleasures to the garden as larger features, yet don't take as much effort or expense to achieve satisfying results.

You can introduce water into a small space with something as simple as a water-filled tub placed in a sunny spot. Be sure to clean the tub and change the water regularly; stagnant water attracts mosquitoes.

To have a small-size water garden with all the elements of a larger feature, you'll need only to devote a few hours of your time and some simple ingredients: a suitable container, a couple of gallons of water, some bog or aquatic plants (you may have to order these in advance from a specialty catalog), and a few fish to help keep the pool clean.

The container: Searching for the right container is half the fun of tub gardening. Any size will do, but to house a standard water lily or lotus, you'll probably need a container at least 18 inches across; a 25-gallon container is a good bet. Dwarf lilies are great for smaller containers, or try a selection of grasses with different foliage colors and textures. A wooden half barrel is an attractive container choice, and usually easy to find. And you can always hide the main container inside a more attractive—but less watertight—barrel or tub. Examples of commercial tub gardens, as well as those that can be recycled from other materials, are shown on the opposite page.

The site: Because a water-filled 25-gallon container is heavy (more than 200 pounds), it makes good sense to

An old-fashioned hand pump is the perfect complement to a barrel pond. Of course, no hand pumping is required here: a submersible pump keeps the water moving.

set up your water garden in its permanent location. Consider placing it directly on the ground rather than on a deck or patio as the pool will have to be drained occasionally. Also, the structure of your deck may not have been designed to hold such a concentrated load.

As you evaluate possible sites, remember that it's important to provide plenty of sunshine: most aquatic plants need at least four to six hours of full sun daily. Keep in mind, too, that your water garden should complement its surroundings; you may want to locate the pool where it will reflect the color from blooming trees and flowers, for example.➤

TUB GARDEN CONTAINERS

Almost anything capable of holding water can—with suitable cleaning, appropriate placement, and a little imagination—become an attractive garden accent pond. Make a tiny tub garden in a bonsai pot. Or give an old claw-footed bathtub new life with a couple of delicately scented lilies and some slender grasses.

Old wooden trough
Found at an auction or in grandpa's shed, an old trough can make a charming garden, as long as you use a water-tight liner.

New watering trough
You can buy a new metal trough, either oblong or round and holding about 170 gallons, at a feed-and-grain store. To help reduce water temperature fluctuation, sink the trough into the ground, leaving a couple of inches above ground to keep water runoff out of the pond. If you live in a warm climate, this can be a year-round installation.

Wooden half barrel
Used barrels should be scrubbed clean and lined, both for water-tightness and to prevent any substances in the wood from leaching into the water. Smaller rocks and pebbles added after planting will hide the tops of pots.

Cast-iron kettle
An old soup kettle may be just the thing for your garden. If it has no feet, you can support it on crossed wooden blocks cut to shape.

Terra-cotta planter
Be sure to plug the drain hole or add a pond liner before planting. Add a bed of gravel to raise plants to the right height.

Filling and planting: Before placing a wooden, metal, or unglazed ceramic container in its permanent location, it's best to line it with a flexible pond liner (PVC or EPDM). Pleat the liner to fit into a curved container, and cut off the excess at the top. A dark-colored material makes the surface more reflective. If you're using a half barrel, consider lining it with a preformed fiberglass shell designed and sized specially to fit inside.

Remember when you're selecting plants that your pond will be small; one lily per square yard of surface area is plenty, along with a few bunches of oxygenating plants or grasses. Overcrowded plants will not give you a satisfying display of foliage or flowers.

With the exception of plants that simply float free on the water's surface, root aquatic plants before placing them in the pool. Plastic pots are best, since they hold up better than clay when submerged in water. For more information, see the planting instructions that start on page 82.

Submerge planted pots in the pool, positioning them so their tops are 6 inches or more under water.

Some plants thrive if their containers are only partially submerged; raise them to the proper height with bricks or overturned pots on the pool's bottom.

Add a goldfish or two, or some mosquito fish, to keep the water free of insects. Don't overfeed the fish, since this could disturb the pond's ecological balance. A tiny fountain jet, driven by a submersible pump, provides visual interest as well as necessary oxygen.

Throughout the season, check the water level, and refill as required. Remove floating debris, and cut away any dead leaves.

In cold climates, place fish in an indoor aquarium for the winter. Ideally, if you have extra room, move the whole garden to a sunny spot indoors as the weather grows cold.

A tub garden requires very low maintenance; simply keep the water level topped and remove any dead leaves as they occur. A fertilizer tablet placed in the pots of blooming plants every three weeks or so will help keep them flowering all season.
Design: Aerin Moore,
Magic Gardens

Water Illusion

Interlocking raised plant and water garden boxes, such as those in the example shown below, are designed to add beauty to an area and to fool the eye. Water appears to fall from the top box, but is actually recirculated from the pond itself by a submersible pump.

The boxes are made of 2x6 decking faced with ¼" cedar, nailed together and bolted to the deck. The pond is lined with 20-mil blue vinyl swimming pool liner, which is covered with 6-mil black polyethylene sheeting. A layer of sand under the liner cushions it and helps keep it from being punctured. An EPDM or PVC pond liner could also be used. The plant boxes are lined with the same black polyethylene sheeting over 10 inches of rock and gravel.

Both water lilies and goldfish thrive in the pond box, while earth-loving plants share the planters.

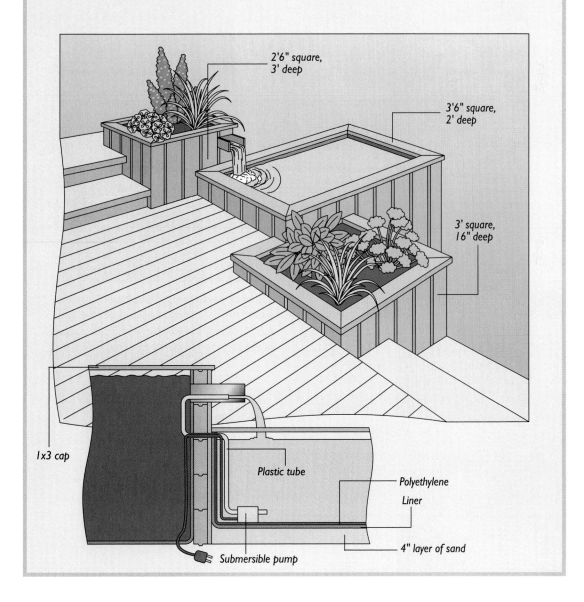

2'6" square, 3' deep

3'6" square, 2' deep

3' square, 16" deep

1x3 cap

Plastic tube

Polyethylene Liner

Submersible pump

4" layer of sand

A Fountain for Every Garden

Water in motion is nearly always dramatic, and a flowing fountain introduces water as a star performer in the garden scene. But in addition to merely entertaining with sound and motion, a fountain does more practical work. It aerates the pond water, providing fresh oxygen to plants and fish. And it benefits people as well, turning the garden into a cool retreat on a hot day, and screening off outside noise and distractions with its soothing musical sounds.

A full, gushing fountain may appear to be an extravagant use of water, but in fact most contemporary fountains are not water guz-

In a small pool, this simple bubbler fountain is a good choice: The thick column of water is easily seen against the rocks (which hide the pump), and there's no overspray to drench guests.

Water for this self-contained splash sculpture fountain is recycled from a basin at the foot of the sculpture, concealed among the foliage.

zlers. A submersible or recirculating pump draws water from the pool and feeds it back to the fountain head or water inlet, where it's used again and again.

Fountains that spray and fountains that spill are the basic types. Versatile spray fountains have heads that send water upward in shapes ranging from massive columns to sprays as delicate as lace. Spill fountains take two basic forms: either simple tiers of spill pans, in which the water first pools at one level before falling to the next, or wall fountains, where the water is raised within or behind the wall and then pours out.

SPRAY FOUNTAINS

A spray fountain uses water in opposition to gravity to create picturesque water patterns, to add interest to a piece of sculpture, or simply to add the sight and sound of falling water to a garden.

Choosing the spray pattern: With a little help from an array of foun-tain heads, water can be sculpted into all kinds of fanciful shapes:

• A short, heavy, burbling column of water from an inlet pipe below the pool's surface.

• A gurgling column of water from an inlet pipe above the pool's surface. This column rises higher than one that begins below the surface.

• A fine, forceful spray coming from an inlet pipe with a spray jet smaller than the pipe's diameter. This spray rises vertically, describes a graceful arc, or rotates, depending

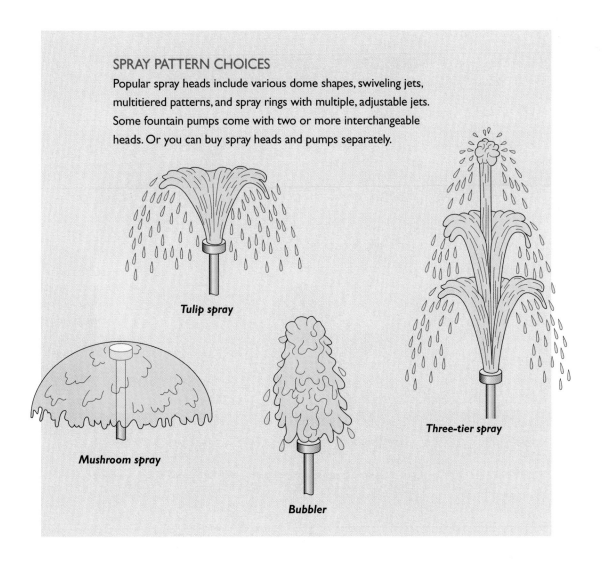

SPRAY PATTERN CHOICES

Popular spray heads include various dome shapes, swiveling jets, multitiered patterns, and spray rings with multiple, adjustable jets. Some fountain pumps come with two or more interchangeable heads. Or you can buy spray heads and pumps separately.

Tulip spray

Mushroom spray

Bubbler

Three-tier spray

upon the fountain head's design.

Design and location: The main rule in spray fountain design is to use a short, heavy column of water in windy spots. Go for height, distance, or drama only where the spray will not blow widely, drenching spectators and wasting water.

Professional designers try to position a spray fountain against a background that dramatizes the movement of the water. In a heavy column, water tends to be translu- cent, so backgrounds ought to be dark. Fine sprays look their best when playing against a flat surface. Heavy sprays tend to dominate and will stand out even against a lacy bower of leaves.

As water rises higher, the pool diameter must also increase pro- portionately; otherwise, a steady loss of pressure will occur as the water level falls, especially in a windy garden. A general rule of thumb is that the basin should be a minimum of twice the diameter of the spray's height.

The fountain jet is usually installed just above the water level; a bubbler fountain *(page 38)* is an exception. If your pool will include water plants or fish, plan the instal- lation very carefully. Many water plants, and especially water lilies, don't like heavy turbulence, and even fish, who benefit from the aer- ation, will likely avoid the immedi- ate area of the fountain.

Multiple holes in this fountain's main head create a mushroom- shaped spray, which is then broken by the scal- loped platform into several small falls.

The curve of the tile-lined lower pool echoes the shape of the spill fountain bowl above it, tying together the two levels of this water garden feature. Matched terra-cotta planters frame the display and bring garden greenery up close.

SPILL FOUNTAINS

Whether a spill fountain is an ordinary household pipe pouring water into a container, a series of spill pans attached to a wall, or a scaled-down version of the great Roman ornamental fountains, it is nearly always designed to capture a specific characteristic of falling water or create a particular effect.

For some people, the simple sound of falling water is adequate; others may want the fountain to carry a symbolic message in its design. Rarely is an attempt made to disguise the water source or to make the fountain appear to be a waterfall. No fountain head is used for a fountain of falling water. Spill fountains, because of their design and sheltered location, aren't normally affected by wind.

Single stream of water: The simplest spill fountain design—and the least expensive—is a single stream of water pouring into a pool or container. The pool can be large or small, depending on the space and budget allotted to it. The classic Japanese *tsukubai*—a hollowed-out bamboo rod trickling water into a stone basin—is a model of simplicity. To save water, add a small submersible pump in a concealed location; a small amount of overflow can feed a bog garden surrounding the pool.

Before the invention of indoor plumbing, wall fountains were practical public water sources. The ancient form is seen frequently in Europe, especially along the coast of the Mediterranean. Townspeople would fill their water jars from water passing through a sculptured figure standing in a wall niche.

Today, the fountain's principal role is ornamental. Water can pour directly into the pool from the pipe, issue from a lion or gargoyle's mouth, or overflow from a basin or series of spill pans or trays.

Styles of spill pans: Spill pans are available in two- and three-tiered plastic or metal sets that you can purchase at home centers or garden supply stores. If you have the necessary skills, you can make a series of spill pans from your own materials and design.

SPLASH SCULPTURE FOUNTAINS

A splash fountain is a spray or spill fountain in which the water's flow is interrupted by a sculpture.

The wide range of designs for splash sculpture fountains suggests a long history. For centuries, pumping water up through a sculpture to splash over a series of surfaces into a pool has been a favored form for fountains. The water inlet was traditionally a Grecian urn or other art object, held by a cherubic nymph or symbolic figure. Nearly every city in Europe has a public square that displays some variation of the splash fountain style. Remember, though, that a formal fountain requires lots of room. If you want to place a splash fountain in a limited space, you can scale down the design. Keep your pool's design in mind as well: Achieving artistic balance with a traditional stone sculpture in a modern pool is tricky; a metal sculpture gives a strong contemporary appearance.

You will find both traditional and modern sculptures in stone and metal at garden supply centers and home centers. Or try a stone-cutting yard or import store. You can commission stone or metal sculptures from artists, at the artist's studio, or at a gallery acting as the artist's agent.

Cherubs are classic water fountain themes, although in this case the water arches from a lily pad rather than from a water jug held in the arms. Large boulders and soft plantings help hide the cast-iron figure from view in other parts of the garden, increasing the feeling of intimacy in this quiet pool area. *Landscape designer: Kathryn Mathewson Associates.*

Cost and construction: Building a formal or classical wall fountain is relatively expensive. Not only is the formal fountain itself a costly project but the surrounding area must have complementary features if the fountain is to suit its environment. It is possible to add a fountain to an existing wall with a submersible pump and water pipes, but construction is much easier if the fountain is built into the wall during initial construction. For more on fountain plumbing, see page 59.

The construction of the raised holding pool is critical, and it's essential that it be done properly. Concrete or concrete block works well, covered with plaster or faced with brick, tile, or stone above the water level. To make a pool watertight, you can also use a flexible liner. For instructions on how to build a concrete pool, see pages 139-140.

This lion head spill fountain looks like an integral part of the wall, thanks to the clinging vines. It's easiest to plan for the fountain—and the necessary plumbing—while you're building the wall.

A new twist on the old theme of spill pans attached to a wall, these spill shelves are supported by reinforcing rods within the core concrete block structure. Bricks and handmade raku wall tiles add a decorative touch.
Landscape designer:
Michael Glassman/
Environmental Creations

Fun Fountains

Pleasing fountains and pools can be surprisingly simple. We show three here, but your own ingenuity may suggest more. Installation is easier than ever before with the ready availability of compact, inexpensive submersible pumps and flexible pond liners. Water and energy costs need not add up: A small pump that circulates 140 gallons of water per hour over a 3-foot drop uses less electricity than a 70-watt light bulb. Begin by choosing a container—or make your own— and make sure that it's waterproof. Then drop in a submersible pump with riser pipe and add water. Any piece of hardware with a smaller aperture than that of the riser pipe can work as a homemade fountain jet: Automotive grease fittings, drip irrigation components, and brass lamp conduit and caps are just three possibilities.

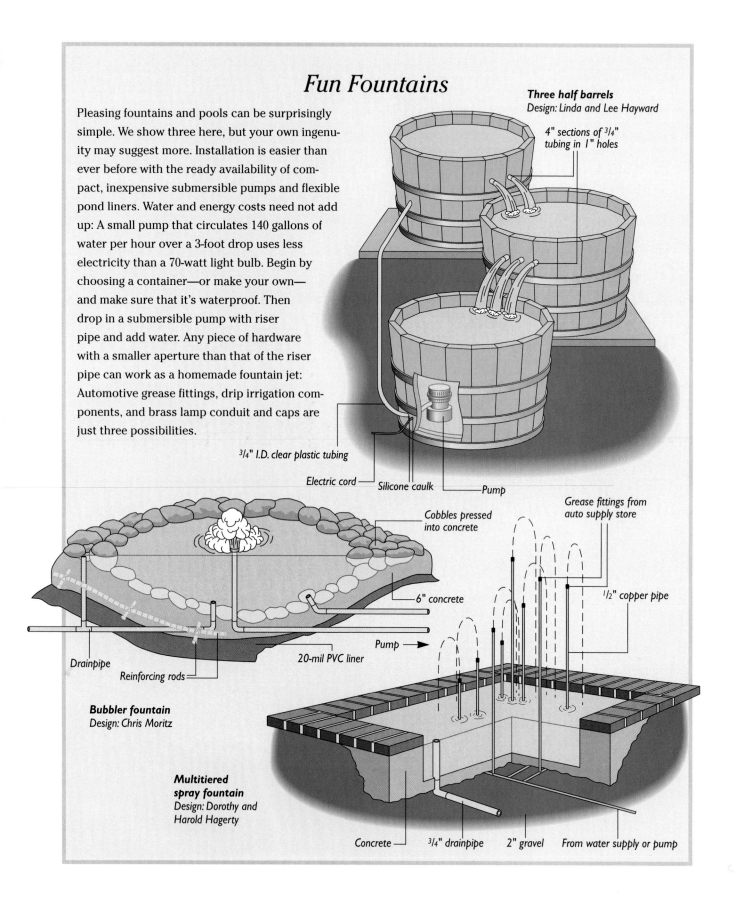

Three half barrels
Design: Linda and Lee Hayward

4" sections of ³/4" tubing in 1" holes

³/4" I.D. clear plastic tubing

Electric cord

Silicone caulk

Pump

Cobbles pressed into concrete

Grease fittings from auto supply store

6" concrete

¹/2" copper pipe

Pump →

20-mil PVC liner

Drainpipe

Reinforcing rods

Bubbler fountain
Design: Chris Moritz

Multitiered spray fountain
Design: Dorothy and Harold Hagerty

Concrete

³/4" drainpipe

2" gravel

From water supply or pump

Waterfall Basics

Whether it's a roaring cascade or a less imposing trickle fall, waterfalls are a bewitching sight, enchanting and inspiring us. It's no wonder that many people have chosen to incorporate this feature of nature into their own yards by combining a waterfall with a garden pool.

Choosing a style: A natural-looking waterfall is just one of your options. Architectural waterfalls—artificial creations using such materials as brick and concrete and tending toward geometric shapes—may be the perfect choice for a formal pool, where it might be difficult to convincingly integrate a natural-looking waterfall.

For ideas, visit nearby public squares, looking for designs to scale down, and study wall fountains you like. Or contact a landscape architect or a designer and ask to see some formal waterfall designs. ➤

WATERFALL STYLES

Whether you want to imitate nature or reflect an urban environment, there's sure to be a waterfall that will look right with your pool. Of course, combinations of these types can work too: You may plan an overhang fall, for example, that empties into the top basin of a stepped fall.

Trickle falls
Even a small amount of water falling a short distance brings the dynamic attraction of moving water to the garden.

Architectural falls
Obviously not natural, the water in an architectural waterfall may pour from one formal pool into another, from the end of a formal stream, or even from a wall.

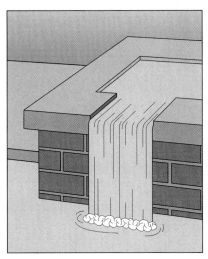

Stepped falls
Water flows through a series of isolated catch basins, possibly of varied sizes. The heights of the falls may vary from one basin to the next. This type of falls still looks good even if the pump is shut down, since water remains pooled in the basins.

Overhang falls
An overhang of several inches is best for a curtain effect; some designers add an acrylic or fiberglass lip to keep water from dribbling down the rock face. The lip is invisible unless viewed from close up.

Many do-it-yourselfers prefer to imitate nature, feeling that a waterfall that looks natural best fits the style of their garden.

The basic idea of this type of waterfall is to create two or more separate pools at different heights so they will appear to have been formed by nature itself. (A torrential waterfall with its source mysteriously placed midway up a property line fence, for example, is likely to strike the viewer as artificial.) The upper pool is usually the smallest of the two, just large enough to create a steady flow of water. The inlet pipe enters below the surface or from a niche among border stones.

Whatever style you choose, remember that properly designed waterfalls don't waste water. As with fountains, what appears to be a never-ending, one-way flow is really only a limited amount of water recirculated by a pump and pipes.

Wherever native stone plays a dominant part in a garden waterfall, make sure you have enough room for your creation. Boulders fill up space quickly. Some stones—mainly shale and other sedimentary types—can be stacked in ways

Part of an alpine garden environment, this natural-looking waterfall requires a large volume of water. But a small-scale version, with perhaps two or three tiers, would be quite effective in a home garden.

Along with the soothing sound of falling water, this fall brings a sense of enclosure to the garden because of its height.

PREFABRICATED PIECES

To make waterfall building even easier, consider using some of the prefabricated components that are commercially available. You can find rocks and boulders made from fiberglass and other materials, preformed units that form the lip of the falls and shape the flow of water, and even precast forms with pools and lips that you can use to build the entire waterfall. Many materials are used, including fiberglass, PVC, and concrete; the naturalness of the effect varies. You can often camouflage the edges with smaller rocks and plants.

---

that look natural. This rarely works well with large stones, such as the granite that is so common in western mountains.

By paying close attention to scale, it is possible to build a small but bustling waterfall from a tiny volume of water. You can arrange fist-sized broken stones to appear much larger. Creative imagination can even make dwarf varieties of native plants look like their standard-size counterparts.

Designing a natural waterfall: How do you lay out a natural-looking waterfall? Rather than trying to create something from scratch, look carefully at the way nature works:

• Stubborn flat rocks fortify the center of the stream, forming the edge of the falls.

• Water rushes along lines of least resistance—between, around, and over the firmly entrenched stones —washing away dirt, gravel, and all other loose material.

• Nature frames the falling water's path with stones cast aside or worn away by the rushing water and with appropriate plantings.

The placement of rocks is what really makes or breaks your fall's character. Irregular rocks in the center of the channel create a rapids effect. A big boulder at the base froths the water up even more. Narrowing the sides of the fall compresses the water, forcing it into a thicker curtain. Gaps, grooves, and other irregularities in the lip create unique patterns.

There are no firm rules here. The key is experimentation, moving a rock here, a rock there until the waterfall looks—and sounds—best.

Relaxing Streams

Streams are as varied as any of nature's creations. There are rushing streams amid granite mountains, lazy streams in upland meadows, and muddy streams through farm valleys, ranging in strength from a tiny trickle to awesome rapids.

Before building a garden stream, it would be smart to settle on a design drawn from an existing landscape. Streams that are based solely on one's imagination tend to encounter a few difficulties with the laws of nature.

Stream characteristics: Water moving at a languid pace will wander through curves, always washing the outside bank. Streams, therefore, tend to grow wider at the midpoint of a curve. They become shallower along the inside because water moves more slowly and silt is deposited along the inside curve.

A fast stream rushes in a straight line, detouring only where rocks bar its path. The rushing water tends to keep such a streambed free of mud.

The choice between a slow- or fast-moving stream depends on the topography of your land and may be entirely governed by the landscaping requirements of your site.

In a private garden, a stream that looks natural ought to provide the kind of flow that your property can handle easily. Unless a stream bubbles mysteriously out of the ground, the rushing water usually has a waterfall as its source. The water must be pumped from where the stream ends (perhaps where it flows into a pool) back to the top of the stream, where it begins its journey again. An architectural stream typi- cally issues from either a spray jet or a wall-mounted inlet.

Stream design: Although a contemporary stream might be walled with angular brick, stone, stucco, or adobe, a natural-looking stream is more likely to be made of hand-packed concrete or fashioned from a flexible liner or preformed fiberglass sections. Disguise concrete by overlaying it with stones or pea gravel; hide the edges of a liner with stones, turf, or border plantings.

Though we think of a natural stream as flowing noticeably down-

The water level in this meandering stream fluctuates with rainfall. Boulders of varying sizes add interest even when the water is low.

WORKING WITH AN EXISTING STREAM

If you are fortunate enough to have an existing natural stream running across your property, you've already saved construction time and expense. But if you want to change the stream in any way, be sure to contact the Depart- ment of Fish and Game in your state. Existing laws govern all changes made to streams and they are very strictly enforced. In most areas, you'll also need to contact your county and municipal planning officials.

hill, most garden streams work best if laid out level or at a very gentle pitch. To negotiate a steeper slope, lower each level section as a unit, connecting the sections with small falls. To create turbulence, decrease the depth of the channel slightly, narrow the banks, or add stones. Always build a deeper channel than you think you need: seasonal runoff can flood low banks. Alternatively, plan an overflow pipe of perforated plastic drainpipe to a well-drained spot, as you might for a natural pond *(page 156)*.

A short drop and a slight constriction add a rush of motion to the tranquil stream shown at left.

Crossing Water

Bridges and stepping-stones do much more than just get you from one side of your garden stream or pond to the other. They also provide a whole new perspective on your water feature, allowing you to view the plants and fish up close, as well as unifying your yard visually and acting as decorative elements in themselves.

BRIDGES

Wood, cast concrete, and quarried stone are the three basic bridge building materials. Wood is the most versatile, lightest, the least expensive, and, perhaps not surprisingly, the most common.

A solid wooden bridge can be built along the lines of a narrow deck, with the joists attached directly to the posts or footings. See page 64 for the basics of deck structure.

If you choose a concrete slab bridge, you can build it right on the spot. Create and install the form, place the concrete, and when it has set, remove the sides of the form. You can leave the bottom of the form on, since it will be below the waterline and never be seen.

Quarried stone is a frequently used bridge material in Japanese-style gardens, but it's tricky to work with for beginners. One way

to have the look of a stone (or brick) bridge over a narrow channel of water is to use a precast concrete culvert to form the structure of the bridge. The stone is then added as a facing.

A bridge that spans more than four or five feet should be supported by a footing at each end. Cast footings directly into holes dug in the ground (use a form if the soil is loose). Set a couple of reinforcing rods into each footing, letting them extend far enough to secure the bridge structure to them. Or cast a post anchor into the footing and secure the bridge structure to it. (A large rock can

BASIC BRIDGE STYLES

Arched or flat, straight bridge designs are the norm, but a zigzagging bridge (called a *yatsuhashi* in Japan) encourages a leisurely stroll.

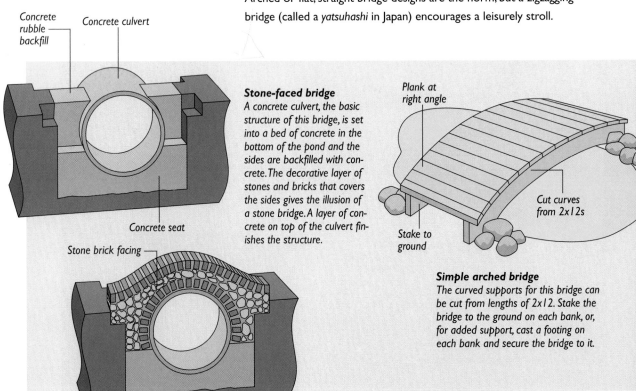

Concrete rubble backfill

Concrete culvert

Concrete seat

Stone brick facing

Stone-faced bridge
A concrete culvert, the basic structure of this bridge, is set into a bed of concrete in the bottom of the pond and the sides are backfilled with concrete. The decorative layer of stones and bricks that covers the sides gives the illusion of a stone bridge. A layer of concrete on top of the culvert finishes the structure.

Plank at right angle

Cut curves from 2x12s

Stake to ground

Simple arched bridge
The curved supports for this bridge can be cut from lengths of 2x12. Stake the bridge to the ground on each bank, or, for added support, cast a footing on each bank and secure the bridge to it.

This gently arched bridge, with its decorative metal railing, blends harmoniously into the garden. The bridge is supported by solid footings well back from the banks of the stream. Be sure to follow local building code regulations for railings.

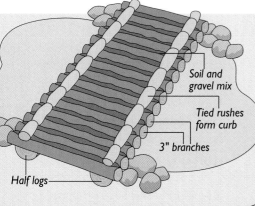

Soil and gravel mix

Tied rushes form curb

3" branches

Half logs

Earth bridge (dobashi)
Made of logs and branches, this simple structure is at home in Japanese-style or other informal gardens. Use straight, evenly sized branches, about 3" in diameter, and fill the spaces between with a mixture of soil and gravel.

Zigzag wooden bridge
Built low to the water, this bridge of wooden decking laid across horizontal supports encourages you to linger. Midspan supports can be sunk directly into the bottom of a natural pond. Or rest each section on its own support column, like stepping-stones.

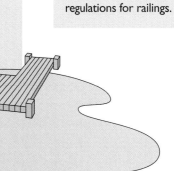

Well anchored at their ends and projecting over the water, these stepping-stones not only look natural, they make crossing this stream safe and easy.

need to install a railing. A railing not only offers safety, it provides strollers something to lean against as they're enjoying the view. For the latter reason alone, you may consider installing one even if it's not required by code.

STEPPING-STONES

More an extension of a path than a bridge, large stepping-stones set just above the water are often the simplest form of small stream or pond crossing.

Materials for stepping-stones include poured concrete shapes, quarried flat stones, boulders, and sliced log rounds. Avoid redwood if you have fish, because it may leach harmful tannins into the water. Examples of materials, and layout, are shown on the opposite page. Clean the stones regularly with a stiff-bristled brush to remove any slippery mosses or algae.

For even greater visual interest, lay stepping-stones at an angle to the two banks or stagger them. Close spacings—based on a short natural step—are safer and induce visitors to linger and enjoy the garden. Stones that are widely spaced encourage a quicker crossing.

support the middle of a low bridge.) When the bridge is in place, conceal the footings with soil, rocks, and plantings. This will help blend the structure into the surrounding landscape.

Make your bridge at least two or three feet wide to promote a sense of security for those who walk across it. A railing that adheres to building code standards is required if the bridge is more than 30 inches above grade. If your pond is two feet deep and your bridge is more than six inches above it, for example, you'll

If your pond is very shallow, consider placing large boulders along its bottom. Each boulder will project above the level of the water, thus creating a natural step. Otherwise, you can support regular stepping-stones on piers built of mortared bricks. It's always best if you plan the layout of your stones as soon as you begin to design your pond or stream. This will allow you to cast the necessary concrete footing for each pier. In a pond with a liner, plan to place a piece of padding material between each boulder or pier and the liner. This will help protect the liner from damage.

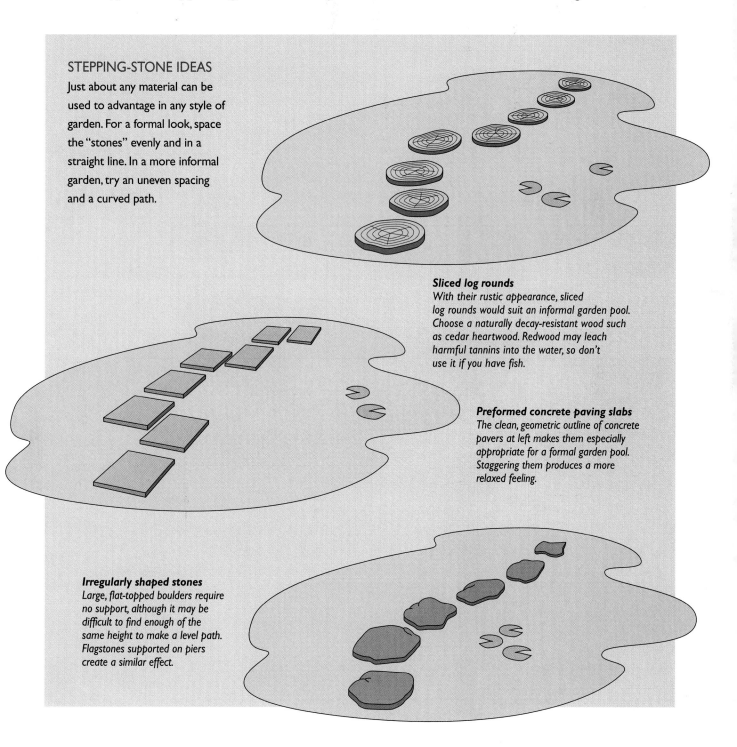

STEPPING-STONE IDEAS

Just about any material can be used to advantage in any style of garden. For a formal look, space the "stones" evenly and in a straight line. In a more informal garden, try an uneven spacing and a curved path.

Sliced log rounds
With their rustic appearance, sliced log rounds would suit an informal garden pool. Choose a naturally decay-resistant wood such as cedar heartwood. Redwood may leach harmful tannins into the water, so don't use it if you have fish.

Preformed concrete paving slabs
The clean, geometric outline of concrete pavers at left makes them especially appropriate for a formal garden pool. Staggering them produces a more relaxed feeling.

Irregularly shaped stones
Large, flat-topped boulders require no support, although it may be difficult to find enough of the same height to make a level path. Flagstones supported on piers create a similar effect.

Planning Your
WATER
FEATURE

Adding a water feature, whether it be a pond, stream, fountain, or waterfall, requires as much attention in planning as it does in building. Before you you start digging, you'll want to consider the location of the feature, the material needed to build it, and whether it will require a pump or filter system. Also, choosing the right edge treatment is paramount in creating a harmonious setting. This chapter will help you make these kinds of early decisions as well as provide a few ideas on lighting the feature and creating structures that will enhance it. If you don't feel that you can handle the work yourself, there's even a section on finding a professional who can help with design and construction.

Whether your water garden is designed on a small scale or is somewhat more elaborate, advance planning will help to balance the various elements. In the garden at left, the wooden bridge and deck complement each other, while the gentle cascade adds visual and aural interest in the background.

Design Decisions

Before you begin work on the pond of your dreams, there are important design decisions you'll need to make. Dealing with these issues from the start should help ensure that your pond is a success.

Before you begin to dig, you'll need to decide what size pond you want, and where it will be located. There are also some legal considerations that may affect the kind of pond you choose to build, and where

you can place it. This section will discuss these and other aspects of the planning process.

Choosing pond size: There will be both budgetary and physical limitations on the size of the pond you

A well-planned combination of forms and colors, and a variety of materials, creates a stunning water garden entranceway.

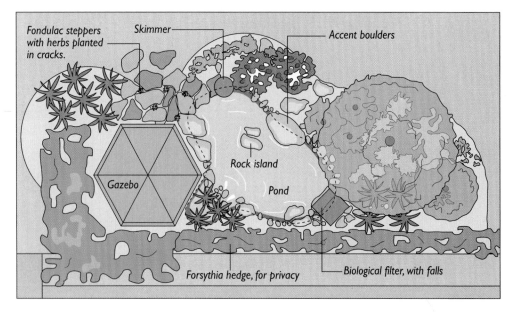

This flexible liner pond occupies a quiet corner of the yard. Rocks and boulders give the edges a more natural look. An extra piece of liner under the rock island protects the main pond liner from damage and a biological filter cleans the water.

Fondulac steppers with herbs planted in cracks.

Skimmer

Accent boulders

Gazebo

Rock island

Pond

Forsythia hedge, for privacy

Biological filter, with falls

have in mind. But when you're considering the range of possibilities that your budget and space allow, there are a number of things to keep in mind.

Although large ponds are more time-consuming to complete—and more physically demanding if you do the digging yourself—as a general rule, they require less work than small ponds once they are installed. In fact, not only is it easier to establish and maintain equilibrium in a big pond, but fish tend to thrive because there's greater temperature stability. Also, a larger pond will leave you the option of adding more fish, or plants for that matter, as you look to develop your creation. Of course, these are not issues for formal ponds with no plants or fish.

You may decide that building a pond on a small scale is the only way to stay within your working budget. Keep in mind, though, that you'll have a difficult and expensive task if you decide to add on to it at some future date.

The role you want the pond to play in your garden will also affect its size. If you want a pond mainly for fish, you can build it to accom-

SAMPLE POND SITES

The yard plans shown at right and opposite are professionally designed pond ideas for two private sites. Although they are tailored to the desires of specific pond owners, they should give you an idea of what to include in your plan.
Designs: Timothy Thoelecke Jr., APLD, ASLA, Garden Concepts, Inc.

Upper pond, biological filter, and falls

Skimmer

Ajuga planted in cracks

The pool in this fairly large backyard is well integrated with the rest of the landscape. The curving shape of the pond and the curving lawn work well together, and the use of rocks and extensive plantings on the opposite side of the lawn helps balance the well-planted pond area.

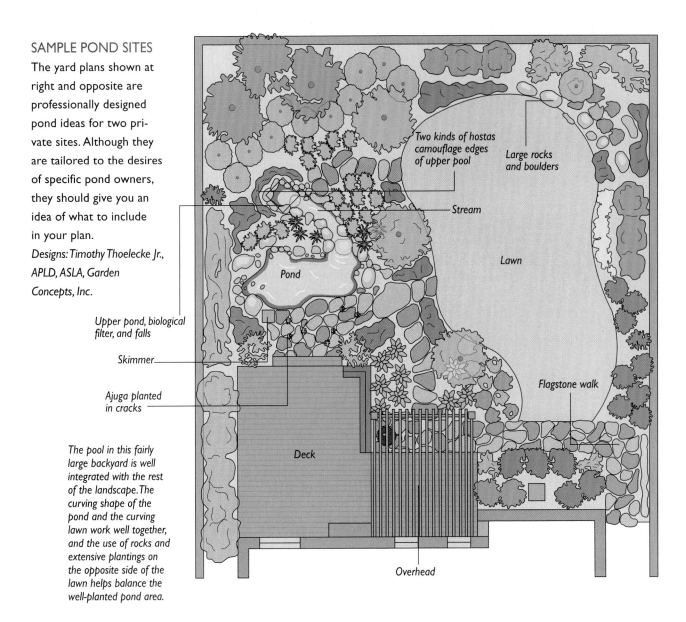

Two kinds of hostas camouflage edges of upper pool

Large rocks and boulders

Stream

Lawn

Pond

Flagstone walk

Deck

Overhead

modate the number of fish you want to stock. Each square foot of surface in a mature pond can support two to three inches of fish (use the ultimate adult length of the fish when making the calculation); in a new pond, calculate for only one inch per square foot. Big, active fish, such as koi, prefer a fairly large pond so they can get enough exercise. If the pond is mainly a garden ornament, build it to the size that suits its surroundings and let that determine stocking levels. And don't forget the space requirements of any external pond equipment, such as a recirculating pump, or a biological filter.

Choosing a location: Deciding where to locate a pond often involves compromise: The place

Debris from trees is not as much of a problem for a large pond like the one above, but skimming the leaves out is still a good idea. The wide deck provides a seat in the shade for contemplating the scene.

Even for a tiny fountain *(right)*, good planning can help the new feature look integrated sooner. Lush plantings here give the impression the fountain's always been part of the garden.

you think the pond might look best may not be the best place for the pond's needs. Discussed below are the various factors that influence the choice of a good pond site.

Most aquatic plants need at least four to six hours of direct sunlight daily (otherwise, they may not grow vigorously or flower), so place a pond with plants to receive the maximum sun possible.

A fairly open area will satisfy the plants' sunlight requirements, but may need protection from wind in cold climates, since many plants, and especially lilies, will not do well in the cold or in moving water caused by wind. For a windbreak, choose something with openings, such as a hedge or a lattice fence.

Trees, although attractive in their own right, are potential problems for a pool. They may create too much shade, reducing the amount of sunlight that gets to your plants. Also, deciduous trees, in particular, tend to drop leaves and other debris, which sink to the bottom of the pool and rot, creating a potential problem for the water quality. One way to reduce this hazard is to skim off leaves regularly, and to cover the pond with a net in the fall. Finally, invasive roots may, over the long term, damage the sides of the pond. Some experts recommend locating the pond a distance out from the tree equal to the tree's ultimate mature height. If space does not permit such a generous margin, try at least to locate the pond out of the shade of the tree, so it gets enough sun. Check regularly for signs of damage.

A pond's proximity to the house may affect its role. Locating it near the house might increase the hours of enjoyment you get from it: A pond may offer a tranquil spot to enjoy a morning coffee, for example, or provide a vista outside the back window. (Visibility from the house can be an added safety factor if you have young children who'll play near the pond.) On the other hand, you may want to tuck it into a far corner of the yard, perhaps even screened from view, in order to create a secluded place for quiet meditation.

When considering a remote site, remember that you'll need plumbing and electricity for your pond, so consider how difficult—and how expensive—it will be to get power and water to the site. ➤

Lush plantings and a small island give this small pond a natural look. Repeated use of a few different plants creates a more cohesive effect than a random scattering of many different varieties.

Existing structures don't have to be a drawback to a pond environment: The weathered barn provides a charming backdrop to this tranquil pool.

The nature of the terrain may also suggest a good location. For example, if your yard has a slight rise, and you want to include a waterfall or stream, it makes sense to take advantage of the natural contours. It'll look more realistic, too, if it follows the real slope of the site. But don't locate the pond in an area where surface runoff collects, because it may be swamped by a heavy rain.

The ground's composition may also play a role in your choice; if it's too hard to dig, or too soft to hold its shape, you might choose another location, or build a raised pool with no excavation.

Legal considerations: Regulations in the area where you live may affect various aspects of your pond's design. In some areas, a pond more than 2 feet deep may need to be ringed with a fence, just as a swimming pool does. Or a bridge over 30 inches above grade may require a railing *(page 67)* that meets building code requirements. It's always best to contact your local building department for more information.

If there's a natural water feature on your property, such as a stream, consider yourself lucky and don't try to change it. Modifications to natural water elements, such as damming or diverting water from a stream, are usually regulated at both federal and state levels. Such modifications, even if minor, can have serious consequences for both flora and fauna. Your county cooperative extension office can tell you the name of the appropriate government office to contact in your area.

Making a detailed plan: Once you have decided approximately what size pond you want, and have located the suitable areas of your yard, it's time to draw up a plan.

Take accurate measurements of your site, and then sketch it to scale on graph paper. Draw in the existing landscaping elements such as structures, planting beds, and trees, and the location of utilities. Sketch in the pond that you think you want, trying different shapes, sizes, and locations until you find a combination that suits you. Mark the location of any external elements that the pond requires, such as a pump or filter chamber. And include any structural or landscaping elements that you'll be adding around the pond.

You should also consider what to do with the earth you dig out to make the pond. You can build a new raised planting bed elsewhere in the garden. Or integrate the earth into the water garden design: Mound it at one end and create a waterfall, or build up the banks around the pond and grow shrubs and other plants. Sketch in these possibilities on your plan.

Finally, you can mark out the possibilities right in the yard, with a length of rope or hose to simulate the outline of the pond. Laying out any new landscape features, such as a path leading to the pool, gives a good idea of the overall effect.

Islands

An island in a garden pond can be a simple pedestal with a statue on it, a small mound with plantings, or an area large enough for a gazebo. (To provide access, you'll need a bridge or stepping-stones, see page 44.)

Perhaps the easiest way to design an island for a flexible liner pond is to include it in the plans right from the beginning. Leave some of the ground in place when you're digging out the original hole, and then drape the liner over it. Don't forget to calculate the extra liner you'll need to cover the island.

Once you've placed the liner, cut a hole in the section that covers the island and finish the edges as you would the edges of the pond. For a natural look, secure the edges of the liner in place with rocks, and camouflage the remainder with small stones and plants. For a harmonious look with its surroundings, plant the island with the same type of plants used for the general landscaping.

Another option for islands is to build a brick or concrete block wall to enclose an area in the middle of the pool, fill the area with earth, and plant on top of it. Essentially, this is a big raised bed built out of masonry materials. Protect the pond bottom under the masonry with an extra piece of liner, and be sure to make your wall waterproof.

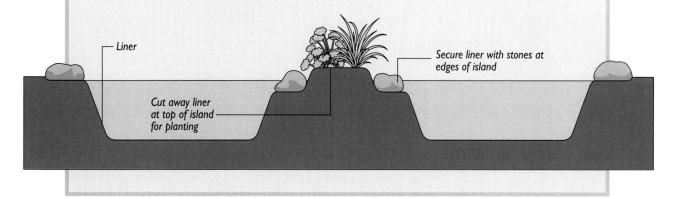

Liner

Cut away liner at top of island for planting

Secure liner with stones at edges of island

Pool Materials

At one time, concrete was the usual material for ornamental pools. Nowadays, a flexible liner or preformed shell is a common choice. The most frequently used materials are discussed below. Installation instructions begin on page 130.

Flexible liners: Widely available in home centers, garden centers, and mail-order catalogs, liners are available in a variety of materials—some longer-lasting than others—and a range of prices. One of the most common choices, and usually the least expensive, is PVC (polyvinyl chloride). The thicker grades last longer and are often guaranteed for about 10 years. However, even the best quality PVC liners become brittle with age, making repairs difficult. They also tend to deteriorate

MATERIAL OPTIONS
Any style of pool—formal, informal, or something in between—can be built with any of these materials. But some combinations make good sense: A flexible liner, for example, is a good choice for an informal pool because it can take any shape at all. But a perfectly circular formal pool would be much easier to create with a preformed shell.

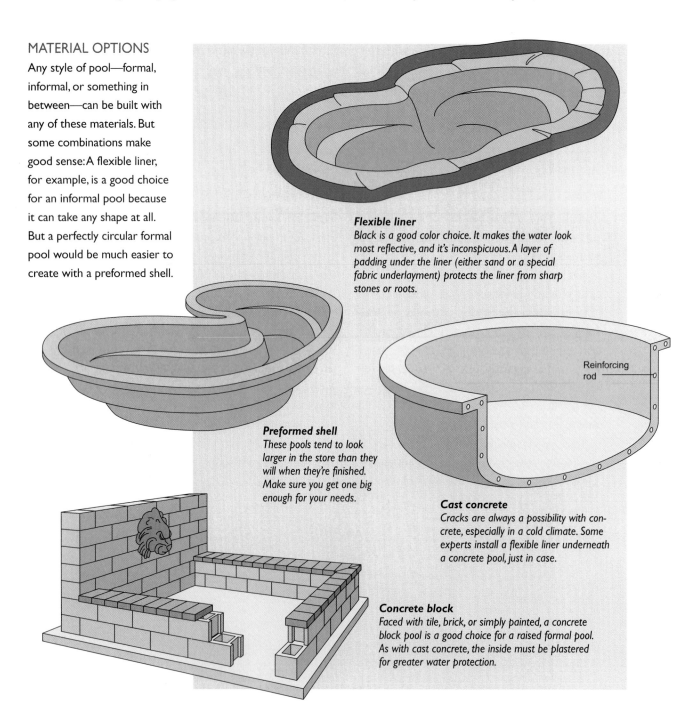

Flexible liner
Black is a good color choice. It makes the water look most reflective, and it's inconspicuous. A layer of padding under the liner (either sand or a special fabric underlayment) protects the liner from sharp stones or roots.

Preformed shell
These pools tend to look larger in the store than they will when they're finished. Make sure you get one big enough for your needs.

Reinforcing rod

Cast concrete
Cracks are always a possibility with concrete, especially in a cold climate. Some experts install a flexible liner underneath a concrete pool, just in case.

Concrete block
Faced with tile, brick, or simply painted, a concrete block pool is a good choice for a raised formal pool. As with cast concrete, the inside must be plastered for greater water protection.

with exposure to the sun's ultraviolet (UV) rays.

EPDM (ethylene propylene diene rubber membrane) is more expensive than PVC, but is generally considered a much better pond liner material. It remains flexible with time, and does not deteriorate with exposure to sunlight.

Be sure that the liner material you choose is specifically intended for use in ponds: Some kinds may contain chemicals that are harmful to pond plants and fish.

Preformed shells: Usually made of fiberglass, although sometimes molded from plastic (polyethylene), preformed shells are available in a range of sizes and shapes, with premolded shelves for plants. Fiberglass shells are more expensive, but

Building a small pond is fairly easy with a preformed shell like the one shown at left. Dig a hole roughly the shape of the shell and then backfill to support the sides and shelves. Disguise the edge with vegetation.

For a steep-sided pool like the one below, one option is shotcrete, a mixture of hydrated cement and aggregate that is shot from a nozzle under pressure to cover a grid of reinforcing rods.

are usually longer lasting and more resistant to damage; they're also fairly easy to repair. A fiberglass shell should last between 10 and 30 years, if properly installed.

Plastic shells, though less expensive, tend to become brittle over time, and may deteriorate with exposure to UV rays. Plastic models may last from 3 to 10 years.

For both fiberglass and plastic, good support is crucial, since the pressure of the water can warp the shell if it's not supported properly. Edging materials must not rest on the lip of preformed shells because the weight can damage them.

Concrete: Cast concrete's main advantage is that it is cast in a prebuilt form, allowing you to create any geometric shapes with perfectly straight lines and squared corners. Its utilitarian character can be disguised either with paint or a facing of brick, tile, or stone. To withstand the pressures of soil and water, the concrete is normally reinforced with steel. The amount and size of the steel depends on the geographical location and the structural requirements. For this reason, get professional assistance.

Other materials: Concrete block, brick, and wood are all possibilities for the structure of a raised pool. It's best to waterproof the structure with a flexible liner.

The greater size of concrete blocks means quick assembly and fewer mortar joints per square foot of surface than other masonry units, and they can be faced with tile, stone, or even brick. Because of their hollow cores, concrete blocks are easier to reinforce than brick.

Decorative tile is a popular choice for formal pools, both inside and out. Tile is often laid over cast concrete or concrete block. Choose vitreous (nonabsorbent) tile for areas in contact with water.

Patterned tiles can dress up a cast concrete or concrete block pond. Adding tiles is a job you can do yourself, similar to tiling indoors.

Pool Hardware

After an initial start-up period, small garden pools may reach a relatively stable environment without the need for even basic hardware. Large fish ponds, waterfalls, and fountains, however, require pumps, filters, and other plumbing components. Some of these are discussed below.

Pumps: A pump serves three purposes in a garden pool: It recirculates water to a fountain or over a waterfall, conserving water and providing the pressure or "head" necessary to pull or push water through the system; it allows you to drain the pool in the event of a leak, or for routine cleaning and maintenance; and it helps aerate the water, adding necessary oxygen and promoting clean water for fish. You'll need a pump to power most pool filters. Adding a T-fitting to the supply piping will allow a single pump to serve more than one pool feature.

Pumps come in two basic types: submersible and nonsubmersible. The best submersible pumps are made from brass and stainless steel; plastic housings coated with epoxy resin are also quite popular.

Submersible pumps may come with a screen attachment, but another option is to place the pump in the bottom of a bucket and then fill the bucket with gravel or rocks; the rocks allow water to pass through but keep large debris out. This method also anchors the pump to the pond floor.

Nonsubmersible pumps are available in two models: high-volume low-pressure or high-volume high-pressure. The former is also called a circulator pump; the latter is the type used in swimming pools. A strainer basket ahead of the pump's inlet prevents leaves and other debris from entering the pump itself.

Submersible pumps are a good choice for part-time use, such as driving a small waterfall or a fountain. Or for full-time use in a small pond, perhaps running a biological filter *(below)*, where they only have to move a small volume of water.

Circulator pumps can handle large volumes of water easily. Swimming pool pumps are generally used only with the largest of pools or when a pressurized-sand filter is involved. The higher pressure is required to pump the water through the filter.

Filters: The three basic types are chemical, mechanical, and biological. Chemical filtration simply means utilizing algicides and other water-cleaning chemicals to attack particular impurities. This method is often chosen for small garden pools with no plants or fish.

Mechanical filters use a straining mechanism and different filter-

Electrical Safety

Whether it's powering a fountain or a biological filter, a pump needs electricity to run. Here are a few tips to keep in mind when working with electricity near water. For more information, see page 166.

• Consult your local building code for any recommendations or requirements.

• Hire an electrician to do the work if you're at all unsure of your own abilities.

• Only use those components that are designed for use in or near water.

• Use weatherproof or waterproof junction boxes where cables connect and locate them above water level.

• Use receptacles that are protected by a ground fault circuit interrupter (GFCI).

• To protect against weather and accidental damage, run underground cables through conduit.

• Cover conduit with a board to reduce the chance of cutting through a cable during future digging.

ing materials to trap dirt particles in water passing through. One variety simply circulates water through a box or cylinder containing activated carbon, zeolite, brushes, or fiber padding. While these devices are economical, they tend to clog easily under heavy service (as in a fish pond), requiring frequent backwashing and/or replacement of the filter agent. Most catalog models can be powered with a simple submersible pump and flow, waterfall style, back into the pond.

Another option is a pressurized-sand swimming pool filter. These filters do require regular back-flushing, in addition to a change of sand (120 pounds or so) every so often.

A biological filter is a variation on the mechanical theme, relying on pumped water to circulate down or up through a filtering agent. The difference is that the filter bed supports a colony of live bacteria that consume ammonia and harmful pathogens, converting it into nitrites and then into nitrates for use again by plants and fish. The system depends on constant movement of water—and thus, oxygen—through the filter to keep the bacteria alive. Without sufficient oxygen, they can start to die in as little as 6 to 8 hours, cutting off the supply of fresh water to your fish. A reliable pump is a must. Some experts recommend a pump with power slightly exceeding your expected requirements. That way, the pump will not be constantly working at full capacity, and if you decide to add more fish or a new feature, you'll have the available power to do so without problems.

Other hardware: To ensure a constant water level, install a float valve, either a special pool model or the toilet tank type. When the water level sinks below a certain level, the valve opens and fresh water enters the pool. Another useful device is a built-in skimmer, which can be cast in place on the side of a concrete pool. And with biological filters, you might want to add a venturi (below).

Installing a drain in your pool provides for easy maintenance. The absence of a drain means the pool must be siphoned or pumped empty for cleaning, making the last mud and water puddles hard to flush from the floor. For information on drains, see pages 160 and 162.

A Venturi for Oxygen

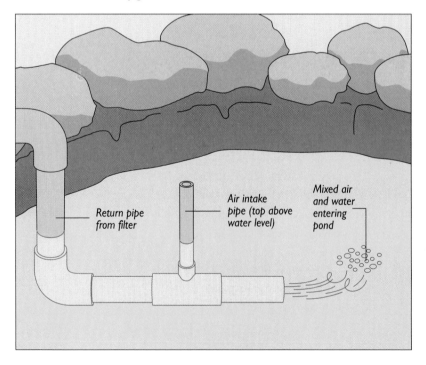

Return pipe from filter

Air intake pipe (top above water level)

Mixed air and water entering pond

Adding a venturi (left) is an easy way to provide extra oxygen for fish. It's especially recommended for a pond using biological filtration, since the bacteria that break down the ammonia consume a large percentage (up to 90%) of the oxygen in the water.

Usually, the venturi is placed at the end of the return pipe bringing water back to the pond from the filter. The water passing through the return pipe causes air to be sucked in through the air intake pipe and mixed with the water when it enters the pond. You can buy a venturi or make one of your own using PVC pipe and fittings.

Borders and Edgings

The borders around a pool are as important to its overall appearance and sense of harmony with the rest of the garden as the flowers and fish that inhabit the water.

There are many materials that can be used as pond borders or edgings, including: grass, whether seed or sod; a bog garden; native stones and boulders; pebbles; river stones; flagstones laid in mortar; a wide concrete lip (which can double as a mowing strip if the pond is next to the lawn); bricks or concrete pavers laid in sand or mortar; tiles; rot-resistant wood, such as cedar heartwood, laid flat or upright in columns; wood chips. Old railroad ties are not recommended because they contain chemicals that may be harmful to plants and fish. And remember, if you have fish, don't let redwood touch the water—tannins that are harmful to fish may leach from it into the water.

Your choice of edging material will depend, to some extent, on

The concrete slab patio overhanging one edge of the pool shown above ties the two elements together visually. Lush foliage and colorful tulips help soften the austerity of the concrete.

the style of the pool and the rest of your garden. Evenly sized, regularly spaced materials, such as bricks or concrete pavers, tend to emphasize the formal aspect of a pond, whereas irregularly shaped or loose-laid materials, such as boulders or pebbles, tend to give a more informal look. Of course, it's always possible to successfully integrate various materials with either type of pool, because the pool's style is the result of the interaction of several different factors such as shape, planting style, and border material.

A formal pool, which is symmetrical and balanced, may be edged all around with bricks, with a second material added for character. In some cases, using more than one border material is a must. You wouldn't want a bog garden around the whole pool, for example, because you wouldn't be able to access the water's edge. A mixture of paved areas and plantings, or various types of edging materials, can help you integrate the pool with its surrounding environment.

The use of different edging materials around the pond helps create two distinct areas in the garden shown at left. The sharply cut corners of the brick edging lend a formal air to the pool beside the flagstone patio. The gentler curves of the concrete give the area bordering the lawn a more relaxed, natural feeling.

You might lay flagstones in mortar next to the patio, or have a grass-edged area next to the lawn.

If you have a sunken pool, especially one without a drain, it's best to add a raised border to keep out runoff when it rains. Likewise, overflow, which can drown nearby plants or wash fish out of the pond, will also be avoided. Even if your pool does have a drain, you wouldn't want the water to be muddied by runoff. A border at least an inch or two above the ground helps prevent mishaps. Materials with thick profiles, such as brick or wood, are best for raised borders.

Putting a drain around the pool should take care of any surface drainage on the neighboring landscape. This is done by first digging a trough around the pool and placing gravel in the bottom of it. Lengths of perforated drainpipe are laid on top of the gravel and the trough is refilled. It's also a good idea to hook up an overflow pipe from the pool. See page 164 for an illustration.

Built in sections to conform to the pool's shape, the wood edging at left forms a comfortable benchlike seat around the raised pool.

The pebble beach at one side of the pool above almost invites waders into the water. The stone edging around the rest of the pool keeps the beach from looking out of place.

Poolside Structures

A water garden will be a beautiful addition to your yard, and one that you'll want to enjoy close at hand. The structures shown in this section—including decks, overheads, and benches—will allow you to do precisely that, but you need to plan carefully, since some of these elements—decks or overheads, for example—will be harder to add once the pond is installed. Even a simple bench can influence how the pond is designed. You might want to orient the pond toward a potential viewer, for example—so it's best to plan for any of these options right from the start.

On these pages, we'll show you the basic design elements of popular poolside structures. Of course, you'll need more information, and in some cases a building permit, so be sure to contact your local building department before you start.

DECKS

A deck can be freestanding or supported by a ledger strip bolted to the foundation, as shown in the illustration below. For a free-standing deck, replace the ledger with a beam, supported by a row of footings and posts.

The basics of deck structure apply to building flat bridges, too. But leave out the joists, and anchor the beams on either side of the water, either directly in concrete or attached to posts on footings.

Decks and bridges more than 30 inches above grade will require a railing (page 67). ➤

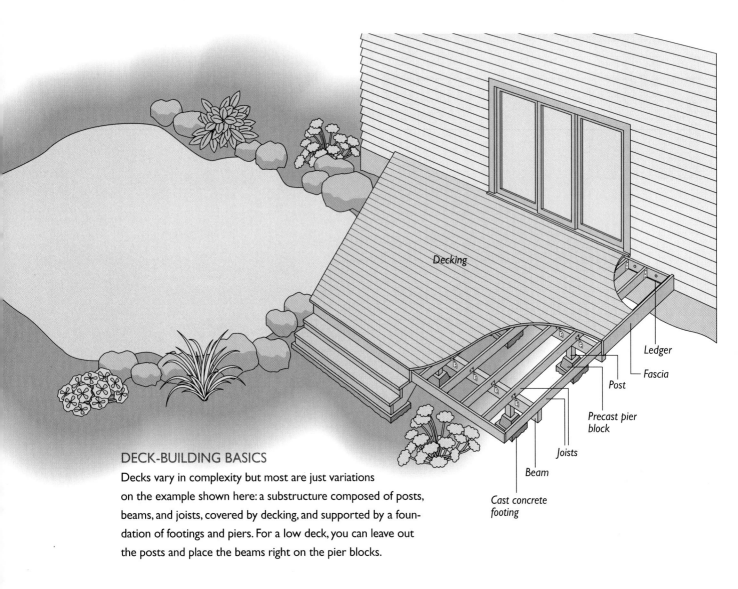

Decking

Ledger

Fascia

Post

Precast pier block

Joists

Beam

Cast concrete footing

DECK-BUILDING BASICS

Decks vary in complexity but most are just variations on the example shown here: a substructure composed of posts, beams, and joists, covered by decking, and supported by a foundation of footings and piers. For a low deck, you can leave out the posts and place the beams right on the pier blocks.

This ample deck provides a convenient spot to enjoy the water garden, while acting as a bridge across it to the overhead and flagstoned patio beyond.

SCULPTING THE EDGES

Rounded edges give this deck a water-sculpted look. *Design: Lorraine McKie and Peter Munnelly*

A deck's corners do not have to be square, nor do its edges have to be straight. A curved edge can give a deck a more "natural" look, allowing it to blend in with an informal pool, where the more typical geometric outlines of a deck may look out of place.

To sculpt the edges of a deck, whether in gentle waves, like the example shown at right, or in one long sweeping curve, let the decking overhang the substructure when you're building, then cut it off freehand to the outline you want with a reciprocating saw. To enhance the water-worn effect, round the edges with a wood rasp and sand them smooth.

The hexagonal overhead at left is the traditional shape of a gazebo, but its open cover gives it a lighter look than the traditional solid roof types, while still providing shade for poolside loungers.

seating area, provided that their posts are anchored in footings.

The structure of an overhead is essentially the same as that of a deck. A ledger strip attached to the house supports one end and posts support the other. Of course, a free-standing overhead will have posts all around. Beams span the distance between the posts and support rafters (the equivalent of deck joists). On some open-style overheads, the rafters are the extent of the roofing. Or you can add a covering of spaced boards, lattice, lath, or solid roofing.

The amount of shade cast by an open cover depends on the thickness and spacing of the material used. Lath or boards laid flat block midday sun but let in more sun in the early morning and late afternoon. Boards set on edge diffuse early morning and late afternoon sun, but let in more light at noon. To design a cover that suits your needs, tack up a few pieces of various materials, placed in different directions and at variable spacings, and observe the shade that is cast throughout the day.

OVERHEADS

The shade that an overhead provides can make the time you spend sitting by your pond on a hot summer day much more enjoyable.

Overheads can be as simple as a post-and-beam structure with widely spaced rafters for a cover, or as elaborate as an octagonal gazebo with a shingled roof.

Although overheads are frequently constructed as an addition to a deck, they can also be free-standing, shading a patio or other

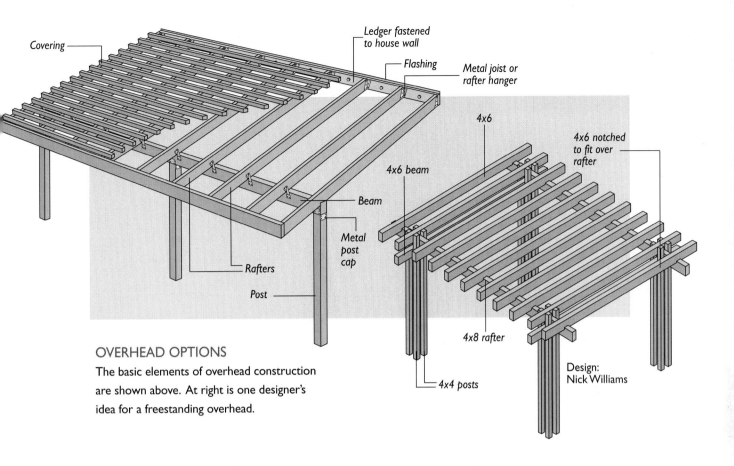

Covering

Ledger fastened to house wall

Flashing

Metal joist or rafter hanger

4x6

4x6 notched to fit over rafter

4x6 beam

Beam

Metal post cap

Rafters

Post

4x8 rafter

4x4 posts

Design: Nick Williams

OVERHEAD OPTIONS

The basic elements of overhead construction are shown above. At right is one designer's idea for a freestanding overhead.

RAILINGS

The wide, smooth cap rail of a sturdy deck or bridge railing is a good place to lean and watch your lazily swimming fish. A railing can make a narrow bridge or a high deck feel safer. And in some cases, a railing is required by building codes. Generally, a bridge or deck more than 30 inches above grade must have a railing.

The minimum height for a railing is usually 36 inches, but a higher railing feels safer. Many people consider 42 inches a comfortable height. Most building codes require that there be no gaps in the structure wider than 4 inches, and that the structure be able to withstand a horizontal force of up to 20 pounds.

If you have small children, try to design a railing that's hard for them to climb. For example, rather than including a horizontal rail at the bottom, as shown below, you could extend the balusters down to the substructure of the deck or bridge.

RAILING BASICS

Regardless of the design, railings have the same basic structure: vertical posts capped by a cross member laid flat, with the space between the posts filled in with horizontal rails, vertical balusters, or both. The post spacing depends on the size of the cap. A 2x4 cap can span 4 feet between posts, while a 2x6 can span up to 6 feet.

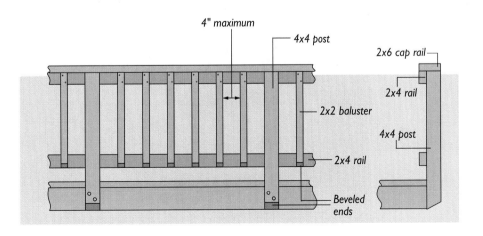

4" maximum

4x4 post

2x6 cap rail

2x4 rail

2x2 baluster

4x4 post

2x4 rail

Beveled ends

BENCHES

Whether you build it or buy it, a bench or chair next to your pool can act as a design focal point, and, of course, as a comfortable seat for pond viewing. Benches and chairs can also be used to separate areas for different activities and to direct foot traffic. A bench can even double as a deck railing. (For a high deck, use a bench with a back.)

Standards of comfort in garden furniture vary depending on what

A bench can occupy a prominent place in a garden or blend in with its surroundings. The classic garden bench above is situated on a raised patio area, making it a central feature of the garden.

The simple curved bench below makes an inconspicuous yet comfortable addition to the yard.

the piece is intended for. Do you want a fairly upright seat to read in or chat with friends, or would you prefer to recline or maybe even take a nap?

For conventional seating, a bench or chair should be between 15 and 18 inches high. Backs should offer support at least 12 inches above the seat. For an inclined back, you'll probably find that the most comfortable angle is between 20° and 30°.

COMFORTABLE SEATING OPTIONS

The classic bench (below, left) is a timeless design that suits a variety of garden styles. The Adirondack chair (below, right) makes a great seat for relaxing. Its inclined seat and reclining back are comfortable, while the wide armrests provide enough room to rest a magazine or a cool drink.

To build a bench that's fixed in one place (either cast in concrete beside a path, or permanently fastened to a deck), follow these simple steps. For a straight bench, saw shoulders in 4x4 posts (A) and set the posts in place. Bolt 2x4 braces (B) to the posts and nail on the 2x6 planks (C). For a corner bench, mark the posts (D), saw shoulders, and add braces (E), then miter the planks and fasten them in place (F).

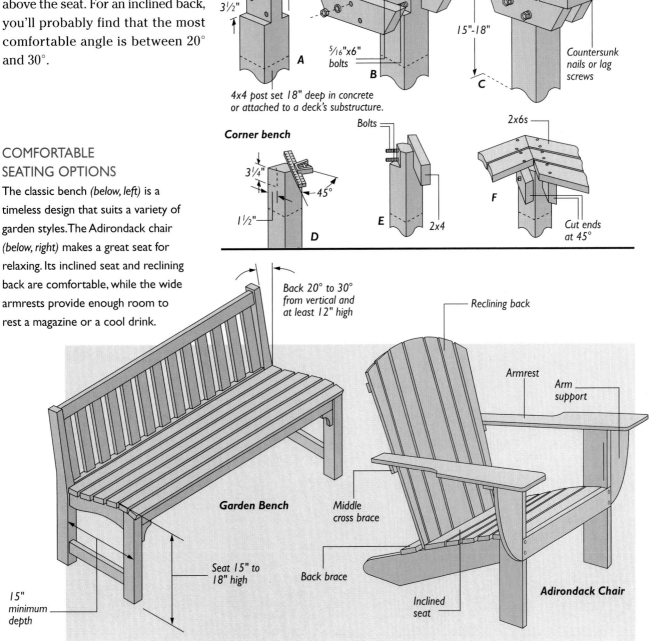

Straight bench

1"

3½"

A

⁵⁄₁₆"x6" bolts

B

Three 2x6s

15"-18"

Countersunk nails or lag screws

C

4x4 post set 18" deep in concrete or attached to a deck's substructure.

Corner bench

3¼"

45°

1½"

D

Bolts

E

2x4

2x6s

F

Cut ends at 45°

Back 20° to 30° from vertical and at least 12" high

Reclining back

Armrest

Arm support

Garden Bench

Middle cross brace

Back brace

Inclined seat

Adirondack Chair

Seat 15" to 18" high

15" minimum depth

Lighting Your Pool

Well-designed lighting in and around your garden pool can make a backyard evening scene come alive. As well, lighting up the night makes negotiating tricky pathways easier, and helps to discourage intruders.

A low-voltage system, which uses a transformer to step down standard household current to 12 volts, is often used outdoors because it's safer, more energy efficient, and easier to install than a standard 120-volt system. They're great for lighting pathways, stairs, the edge of a pond, or even waterfalls. You'll find a selection of fixtures at electrical supply stores. Kits are sold at home centers or hardware stores.

A standard 120-volt lighting system has some advantages outdoors: the buried cable and metallic fixtures give the installation a look of permanence, and light can be projected a great distance. If you want 120-volt lighting, it's always best to plan for it before installing the pool.

A range of outdoor surface fixtures is available, from uplights and spread lights to downlights that are anchored to the house or to trees. Downlighting is good for pinpointing special features; use uplighting to accent or silhouette foliage.

Fixtures for use in the water may be designed to be recessed in a concrete pool wall, or have heavy plates that anchor them to the bottom of a pool or stream. You can even find lights that float on the surface of the

Subtle lighting under the overhang adds sparkle to this sheltered architectural fountain *(above)*.

Underwater lights accent the aerating jet at left, while the falls near the house are lit from below with a portable, sealed light fixture. *Architect: The Steinberg Group. Landscape architect: Eldon Beck Associates*

pond, casting a soft glow. Fountain units may come with their own lighting systems, sometimes with optional colored filters.

Whether you choose surface or submerged lighting is a matter of taste. Surface lighting can be adjusted with more subtlety and precision, and fish and plants tend to look best when illuminated from above. But underwater lights can produce dramatic effects, especially on moving water. The two types can also be combined for dramatic effects. For help creating an overall lighting scheme, consult a landscape designer or architect.

Lighting up structures can add to your evening enjoyment of a pond. The bridge at right seems to shine from within, enticing strollers across to the warmly lit gazebo. *Architect: Mark Hajjar. Pond consultant: Paul Cowley/Potomac Waterworks*

The formal symmetry of this pond is even reflected in the lighting: Four underwater uplights focus on the fountain, while each of the two concrete trickle falls in the background ends in a pleasant glow. *Landscape architect: Talley, Boughton, & Takagi*

Getting the Job Done

Planning, designing, digging, and installing a garden pond is a lot of work, but there's nothing that says you have to do it all yourself. There are many qualified landscape designers, landscape architects, and contractors who can help you along the way. And working with a professional is not an all-or-nothing proposition, either. For example, you could have a landscape architect plan the pond and landscape for you, and then install it yourself; you could design the pond yourself and hire a contractor to install it; or you could design and install the pond yourself, but hire a contractor to build the deck you envision with it.

Regardless of how much work you want to handle yourself, you can choose from a variety of professionals for help and advice. Here's a brief look at some of the trained people who can help you and at what they do.

Landscape architects: Specialized in outdoor structures, these state-licensed professionals can work with you to help set objectives, analyze the site, and produce detailed working plans. If you want a deck, gazebo, or other structure with your pond—they also choose the plants for the site—a landscape architect would be a good person to consult. Some will also oversee the project, negotiating bids from contractors and supervising all the actual work.

Landscape designers: A landscape designer will often have a landscape architect's education and training, but not a state license. They can generally offer the same services as landscape architects, and they're often more experienced

---

POND BUDGETING

Even if you decide to get a professional's help with your project, you'll probably want to calculate the cost of building the pond on your own. That way, when you're discussing prices with a contractor, for example, you'll have a better idea of the potential price range of what you want. Listed below are some tips and pointers to think about when budgeting; they apply regardless of who will be doing the work.

• Buy materials of the highest quality you can afford. Not only will you get long-term durability, in many cases they'll function better even in the short term.

• Prioritize your desires, and build your project in stages, if required. If your plan includes substantial landscaping of your yard, divide it up into smaller segments and install one at a time as finances allow. Even if it's a fairly small project, it may be better to purchase better-quality products for the initial installation, and add desired extras later.

• Keep your ultimate goals for the pond in mind when you're purchasing equipment. It'll be cheaper in the long run to buy a slightly more expensive, but bigger, pump in the first place than to buy a smaller, cheaper pump and have to replace it in a few years because

you want to keep more fish. The same goes for the size of the pool itself: building it bigger from the start is easier, and usually cheaper, than adding on later.

• Consider the cost of border and edging as part of the basic cost of the pool. Other structures, such as a bench or overhead, can be part of a later installation, if your budget can't handle everything at once.

• Investigate the cost of renting equipment, such as a backhoe for digging, and include it in your calculations.

• Don't forget to include the cost of fish and plants in your calculations. This cost can vary greatly, depending on the varieties you select. With fish, as with other pond elements, you can decide to start small for budgetary reasons, and add to your stock over time.

• If you live in a cold climate, figure in the cost of keeping your fish over the winter. You may decide to move them inside, in which case you'll need the appropriate facilities indoors, or you may be able to find a pet store where you can overwinter them.

• Don't forget the cost of such things as baskets for planting, skimmers for removing leaves, a net for catching fish, and possibly a holding tank to contain them outside the pond.

with residential projects. Designers may be certified by their professional association.

Landscape contractors: Licensed landscape contractors specialize in installing landscape elements: paving, pools, plantings, and the like, although some have design skills and experience as well. They usually charge less for design work than landscape architects do, but some contractors may make design decisions based on ease of construction, rather than esthetics.

Contractors hired to build a small project may do all the work themselves; on a large project, they assume the responsibility for hiring qualified subcontractors, ordering materials, and seeing that the job is completed according to contract.

Structural and soils engineers: If you're including any structures with your project, your building department may require that you (or your designer) consult a structural or soils engineer. An engineer's stamp may be required if the structure is to be built on a steep lot, or on unstable soil, for example.

Working with a professional: If you decide to enlist a design professional's assistance with your project, remember that a garden pool and its surrounding landscaping is a fairly permanent addition to your property. You're going to have to live with it for some time, so try to be as clear as possible about what you want—or don't want—so you don't end up surprised with the final result.

Part of the process of working with a designer is communicating your ideas to him or her. Give the designer as much input as you can about the materials, structural elements, plants, and color scheme you would like to have in your garden. An indication of what you're willing to spend will also be helpful. The designer will then develop a working plan based on your ideas—and budget—which you can modify together to arrive at a plan that suits you. Keep in mind that every designer has a personal style; try to inspect a designer's previous work, to see if other projects they've designed suit your taste. If not, consider choosing someone whose style is closer to your own. More tips on working with professionals are offered below.

FINDING GOOD PROFESSIONAL ASSISTANCE

Finding a competent person to do the work is not always easy. Below are some suggestions for finding the right professional for the job and then making sure the work gets done to your satisfaction.

• Ask friends and neighbors to recommend someone who's done work for them. There's nothing like a personal recommendation from someone whose judgment you trust.

• Ask the professional for references from former clients. Call these people to ask about their level of satisfaction with the work, whether the job was done on time, whether it came in on budget. If possible, arrange to visit the sites to inspect the work firsthand.

• Choose someone who's a member of a professional association. Membership does not guarantee quality, but it does indicate a willingness to conform to the rules and regulations of the organization, and to submit to peer review. In some cases, the association has a system for dealing with customer complaints, so you might have recourse if you're dissatisfied. Contact the American Society of Landscape Architects (ASLA) or the Association of Professional Landscape Designers (APLD) for referrals to professionals in your area.

• In order to compare work, and quotes, always interview more than one professional.

• Don't make your selection based on money alone: look for a reasonable cost that you can afford, coupled with good credentials and references.

• Always draw up a contract. Include the names and signatures of both you and the professional; the address where the work is to be done; specific descriptions of the materials and work involved; the agreed time schedule and payment plan. A contract protects both you and the professional, minimizing the chances of misunderstandings later.

Planting
YOUR WATER GARDEN

*Gardening possibilities multiply instantly when
a water feature is added to a landscape. Indeed, once a
pond is installed, most conventional gardeners find
themselves amazed by the number of new options
at their disposal. In contrast to their long-accustomed
problem of having to provide adequate drainage
for plants, they suddenly enter a world where the
vast majority of flora thrives right in water.
The choice of plants alone—from strikingly diverse
lilies and symbolically rich lotuses to tall grasses
and graceful willow trees—is cause enough for wonder.
The following pages will guide you through the planning
process, the selection of the plants, growing them successfully, and propagating them. This chapter ends with
a comprehensive plant encyclopedia, providing a palette
of possibilities to help you create your own
aquatic masterpiece.*

This large pond is a striking example of the rich
diversity possible in a
water garden. Clusters of
lilies dot the surface, while
border plantings range
from the delicate flowers
and grasses in the fore-
ground to robust willows
on the opposite bank.

Planning for Plants

If there is a cardinal rule for all prospective water gardeners, it is this: Plan *before* you plant. By doing this, you have a good chance of achieving gratifying results. Gardens put together on a piecemeal basis tend to contradict important principles of design and usually end up looking disorganized. To avoid this, consider these rules of thumb.

Laying out the site: The key to success here is to determine the garden's main viewpoint, that is, the place from which it will most often be observed. To allow the clearest view of the water, situate large-leaved and taller plants, as well as shrubs and grasses, to the rear of the pond. Smaller plants and flowers should be placed in front.

Plant selection: Choose plants that will make attractive color and profile combinations and give the garden a feeling of unity. Consider the mature size of each plant or tree as you plan its location. A small water feature can easily be overrun by a few fast-growing varieties or obscured by a large tree or shrub. Likewise, small plants can be choked by one or two

Even the simple elegance of water lilies floating in the pond aren't enough to hold attention in this water garden, where the marginals and shrubs provide a dramatic, exuberant display.

rapidly spurting neighbors. Also take into account the blooming season of each plant. With a bit of forethought, you can design your garden to provide an attractive burst of color throughout much of the growing season. It is a good idea to reserve at least a third of the garden for evergreen plants, particularly in colder climates. These will provide a nice visual background in winter, when the rest of the garden lies dormant. When deciding on plants, choose quality over quantity. Ponds packed with a vast array of species often end up looking like a jumbled mess. Select only the plant types that will help achieve the particular effect you want to create.

Sizing up the area: Before deciding on the number of plants, calculate the surface area of the pond *(see page 158 for help)*. This information will come in handy when purchasing floating plants. For proper light penetration, and to allow harmful gases such as carbon dioxide to escape the pond, these plantings should cover no more than two-thirds of the surface.

At some point in the planning process, it's a good idea to make a perspective drawing of the water garden, arranging all-important features such as plants, trees, shrubs, paths, and fences in their desired locations. Even the most rudimentary sketch can serve as a rough planting plan and give you some idea of what the garden will look like when finished. The plant encyclopedia *(page 88)* will help you choose the plants for your garden, but it is first necessary to recognize the various types of plants that populate the balanced pond. The following pages will provide an introduction.

Pool plants are grouped based on their locations in and around the pond. Here are the main types:

Floating plants: These are divided into two basic types: those with their roots in the soil and their leaves floating on the surface; and those whose roots simply dangle

WATER GARDEN PLANTING PROFILE

The different depth requirements of various types of water garden plants are accommodated with shelves or concrete blocks. For easy removal and for rearranging, plants that root in soil can be kept in planting baskets or buckets. The marginal pocket, a mini-bog-garden, at the side of the pool is created by installing a rock dam on the pool side of the marginal shelf.

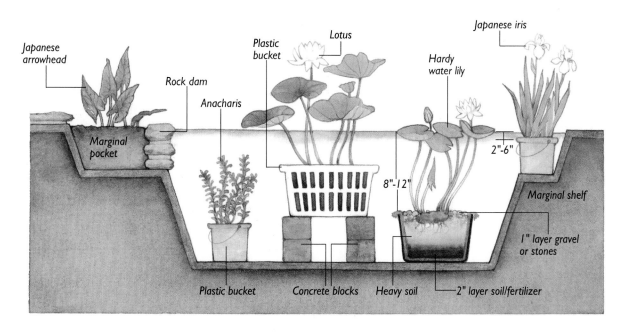

A trio of water lilies gives the pond at left a dazzling burst of color.

In the photo shown below, floaters provide a surreal carpet of green while soaking up toxins to keep the water healthy for the other pond life.

in the water, such as water hyacinth or water lettuce.

The rooted varieties, sometimes called semifloaters, are known for their beauty—the lily being the most obvious example. But they also serve an important ecological role, providing shade for the pond and crowding out competing algae. They don't like heavy turbulence, however, so plant them away from the splash of a waterfall or fountain. Water lilies are discussed in detail on the opposite page.

True floaters grow and multiply with great speed, spreading over open water in very short order. In fact, when water hyacinth was introduced to certain waterways in Florida, it grew so quickly that it became a menace to navigation. On the other hand, water hyacinth is considered an excellent purifier, soaking up ammonia and other potential toxins. (For more information about water chemistry, see page 176.) As much as possible, try to keep floating plants away from

koi; these fish will uproot and shred the roots, which in turn will clog the pond's pump.

Oxygenating plants: These hard workers grow submerged beneath the pool's surface. Blooming as small flowers above the water, they are indispensable to a balanced garden, taking in carbon dioxide and releasing oxygen necessary for the survival of other plants and fish. You can often see tiny oxygen bubbles clinging to the surfaces of these plants. Oxygenators also pro-

Colorful marginals and pond-side plantings help define the water garden environment. Water irises, shown at bottom right, are a natural with natural pools. By planting these in containers, they can be moved to create new arrangements in different areas of the pool.

vide a safe spawning area for fish and a hiding place for their small fry until they are big enough to fend for themselves.

Marginal/Bog plants: Some plants do best around the pool's margins, with their "feet" in shallow water and their "heads" waving in the breeze. Most marginal plants prefer water that is two to six inches deep. These plants benefit from a separate shallow area or a series of shelves around the edges. From a design perspective, marginal plants help provide a smooth transition from the pool to its borders in both formal and natural garden pools and serve to link the pool with the surrounding landscape.

Bog plants are marginals which prefer to grow in wet ground rather than in standing water. They are useful for concealing the materials used to build the pool. They also serve to extend the water environment and make the pool look larger than it really is.

Bog plants often originate from other plant families found at large

in the garden—for example, primrose, lobelia, and calla lilies.

Water lilies: Is it any wonder that lilies are found in the vast majority of water gardens? Stunningly beautiful, dependable, and easy to plant, these semifloaters are the esthetic showpieces in any pond.

Lilies come in hardy and tropical varieties. Hardy varieties bloom

during daylight, opening at about 10 a.m. and closing after sunset. These are the easiest for the beginner to grow and can overwinter in the pool. Tropicals include both day and night bloomers. They tend to be larger and more prolific bloomers, and are available in a selection of varieties and colors. Tropical lilies must be considered

The hearty clump of ferns in the foreground suggests a lush, natural landscape; the random cluster of lotuses farther down the stream completes the image.

The Japanese maple makes a comely addition to the water garden, particularly when it is planted closely enough to be reflected in the pond.

annuals in all but the balmiest climates. With some effort, however, they can be stored carefully over the winter in a greenhouse or other cozy spot.

The best tropicals will bear up to three times as many flowers as hardy varieties. Most flowers live four days once open; just as long as if they'd been cut. To keep lily blooms open for display in your home, use an eyedropper to apply melted paraffin or candle wax around the base of the stamens, petals, and sepals.

Don't be disappointed by a lily's earliest spring blooms. They tend to be smaller and less colorful than the ones that arrive during the summer. To learn more about planting and propagating lilies, see pages 85 and 87. To learn about some of the most popular varieties, see the section that begins on page 91.

Moisture-loving plantings: As a visual feature of the backyard, the water garden stretches far beyond the pond itself, taking in the trees, grasses, and shrubs that make up its background plantings. The best trees to consider are those that love the water and have a light canopy of leaves. These will flourish at pondside and provide some shade but won't drop tremendous amounts of leaves into the pond. Several good species are shown in the section on pages 98 and 99.

As with plants and trees, there are many types of shrubs that thrive beside the pond. With proper trimming, these can become handsome architectural features of the garden, complementing the structure of a formal pool or balancing the bucolic effect of a natural pond. Not to be overlooked, moisture-loving plants such as ferns and grasses are important to any design. These help create a lush pondside environment and prevent soil erosion at the edge of the water. Resist the temptation to cut them back in winter—sparkling with morning frost, they can offer an interesting dimension to an otherwise bleak winter backyard.

Planting Techniques

Planting a water garden is fun—there's none of the heavy work required by a conventional garden. This section gives you the techniques you need to get started. For information regarding specific plants, see the Plant Encyclopedia.

The best time to plant your water garden is during the growing season, from late spring to late summer. If you've just built a pool, let the water age at least a couple of days before planting.

Containers: In pools less than two feet deep it is possible to plant directly into soil at the bottom of the pool, but that will limit your ability to move the plants later. Today, most water gardeners prefer to use movable containers that allow easy rearrangement of plants and quick removal when it's time to clean the pool. For best results,

use containers made from rot-proof plastic. These are typically perforated on the sides to allow the plant's roots to better obtain nourishment from the pond. If you use large-weave plastic baskets—with large gaps—you will need to line them with woven plastic or hessian. This technique is shown on page 84. Solid-sided containers can also be used, but the lack of aeration will stunt growth. This may be desirable if you want to control the growth of a particularly greedy plant that threatens to monopolize space in the pool. Solid-sided containers are also recommended if you keep large, valuable koi, which could injure themselves against the rough edges of a perforated basket. In general, use the largest containers you can. They are easier to move and less liable to tip over.

The number of plants you put in each container will depend on the type of plant. Lilies, for example, should each have their own basket so that the leaf pattern of each plant is displayed to its best advantage, while up to eight oxygenators can occupy the same container. Marginals fall somewhere in between, depending on their size.

Soil: Use high-grade potting soil without organic amendments for water plants, avoiding sandy or limestone-rich earth. Also don't use peat composts; they will float out of containers and increase the acidity of the water, endangering fish and plants. Generic fertilizers and manures are also to be avoided as they tend to cloud and pollute the water. Special fertilizers are available for water plants. Check with a local supplier for more information.

Planting a Floating Plant

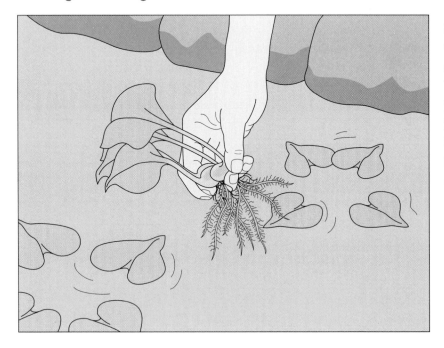

For floating plants, such as the water hyacinth shown at left, simply place them in the water. The only trick is in estimating the number of floating plants you will add to the pond. Within a few months, even a few plants will multiply quickly and provide ample cover for a medium-size pond

Planting an Oxygenator

1 Filling the basket
With a trowel, fill a perforated planting basket with soil. Stop just short of the rim and level the soil across the container with your hand.

Lead strip

2 Inserting the roots in the soil
Decide how you will space the plants in the basket (one 13" square basket can hold up to eight oxygenating plants). Then use your finger to dig a small hole for each one. To weight the plants, place a rock over the bottom of the stems (plants purchased at an aquarium supply store usually come with stems wrapped with a small strip of lead). Insert the first oxygenator into a hole *(above)*. Spread the roots out, then pack the soil to hold it firmly in place. Repeat for the remaining plants.

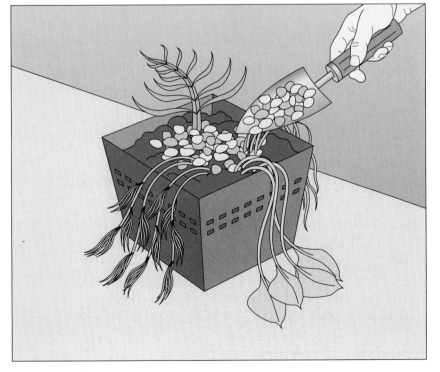

3 Topping up the basket
Once all the plants are in place, use a trowel to top up the basket with stones or gravel. This will keep the soil from leaking into the water and prevent fish from disturbing the plants. Finally, place the container on the bottom of the pool.

Planting a Marginal

1 Installing a liner
Follow the same instructions as for planting an oxygenator *(page 83)*. If you use a large-weave container, cut a piece of hessian or plastic liner larger than you need. Tuck it into the basket, folding the overlap over the edge of the container *(above)*.

2 Adding soil and the first plant
Fill the container with topsoil, pressing the liner snugly against the sides as you go. Carefully remove the first marginal from its pot and stand it upright at the correct planting depth in the soil.

3 Adding the remaining plants
Set the remaining marginals into the pot, then add soil around the plants and tamp it down. With a trowel, top up the container with a layer of stones or gravel.

4 Finishing the job
When you are finished planting the container, trim the liner flush with the edge using a pair of scissors. Place the container in the pool.

Planting a Tropical Water Lily

Crown

1 Inserting the plant in the soil
Do not allow the lily to dry out as you plant it. Keep a watering can on hand and douse the plant periodically if necessary. Fill the basket nearly to the top with soil, then lay the roots in place. To allow for proper root growth, plant the tropical lily at the center of the pot. Hardier lilies can be planted near the edge. Continue adding soil and tamping it until the plant is snugly in place. Be careful not to bury any part of the stem. It is crucial that the lily's crown be above the soil.

2 Covering the soil and placing the plant in the pond
Cover the soil with a layer of gravel or rocks to hold the lily in place (right). Then place the container at the correct depth in the pool. For the best growth, place the container on blocks so that the leaves float on the surface, then gradually lower the pot as the lily begins to grow. Allow a minimum of 3 square feet in the pond for each lily.

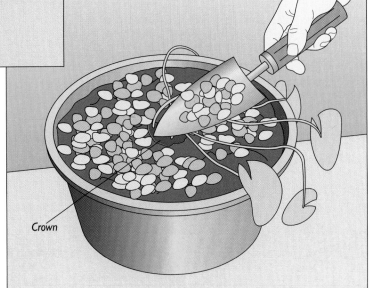

Crown

CREATING A BOG GARDEN

The bog garden has gained great popularity in recent years, and it's easy to see why. Essentially a moist, swampy area, the bog is home to a wide range of stunning plant life.

Creating a bog garden in your pond can be as easy as setting a pot in the water with its lip just above the surface. A more common method is to partition off a "pocket" on the border of the pond using a stone or brick dam. This pocket is then backfilled with heavy soil or gravel and planted. The splash from the pond should be enough to supply moisture. If not, you may have to install an overflow pipe to draw water from the pond. The diagram at the bottom of the page provides a good visual guide.

In general, marginal plants should occupy the wettest area of a bog garden, with moisture-loving plants placed on higher ground at the boundaries. Use the Plant Encyclopedia beginning on page 88 to help you select plants. Don't be afraid to experiment, however, as many plants not designated as bog varieties flourish in these conditions.

The border between pool and garden is blurred by bright moisture-loving bog plants like the striking iris in the foreground at right.

Rock dam

PVC pipe

Flexible liner

Backfill with soil

A BOG GARDEN

Building a rock dam is one simple way of creating a bog garden. Backfill the area with soil, install a pair of short overflow pipes to collect water, then add the plants. For adequate water retention, the flexible liner must extend all the way under the bog area. If soil seepage into the pond is a concern, cover the soil in the bog with a layer of sand or gravel. Alternately, line the inside face of the rock dam with plastic liner.

Propagating plants yourself is a great way to ensure a full and healthy water garden and save a bit of money in the process. Properly cultivated, a single plant can last several generations. Apart from growing them from seed, plants can be propagated in many different ways. Two of the most commonly used methods—by cuttings and by root division—are shown below. The Plant Encyclopedia *(page 88)* lists other techniques for the plants shown; it's best to contact your local nursery for the proper procedures.

To ensure good growth when propagating with cuttings, dip the cut ends in fungicide or dust them with charcoal to prevent fungal attack. When dividing plants, separate them every three to five years. Throw out the oldest parts —they're likely past their prime.

Propagating by Cuttings and Root Division

Taking a cutting
Hold the plant in one hand and pinch off the top of the stem between your thumb and finger *(inset)*. To start the stem cutting, simply stand it in a pot filled with moist soil *(right)*. Once the plant is established, it can be added to the water garden. It's best to take stem cuttings in spring to allow the plant ample time to take root during the growing season.

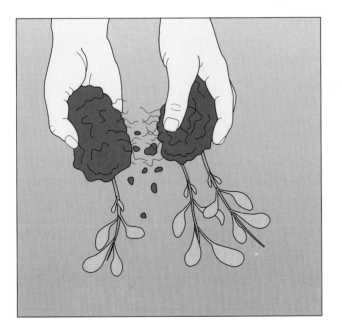

Dividing a root mass
Holding the root mass loosely in your hands, gently divide the plants, making certain each one has its own bundle of roots *(left)*. For stubborn roots, insert two forks back to back and pry the roots apart; firm the plants in moist soil *(above)*. As with stem cuttings, it's best to divide plants in spring.

Plant Encyclopedia

Armed with proper planning and planting information, you are ready to begin the adventure of water gardening. Beginning on page 90, the Plant Encyclopedia features more than 80 plants suited to life in and around your garden. Along with a photograph, each entry contains planting hints, height, and appearance information as well as the best method of propagation. Finally, each plant is assigned a climate zone number, representing the coldest climate in which it will flourish. Use the map below to

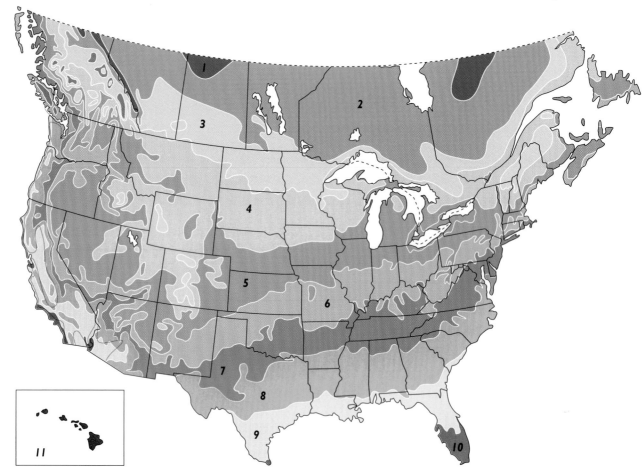

CLIMATE ZONES

This map will help you determine which water plants will grow in your area. The zones are based on average expected low temperatures. To use the map, locate the zone in which you live, then consult the plant listings beginning on page 90 noting the zone number or range given for the particular plant you're considering. The listings indicate the hardiness zones for which each plant is adapted. If your zone falls within the given range, the plant should grow in your region.

	Zone	Temperature
	Zone 1	Below -50°F/-46°C
	Zone 2	-50°F/-46°C to -40°F/-40°C
	Zone 3	-40°F/-40°C to -30°F/-34°C
	Zone 4	-30°F/-34°C to -20°F/-29°C
	Zone 5	-20°F/-29°C to -10°F/-23°C
	Zone 6	-10°F/-23°C to 0°F/-18°C
	Zone 7	0°F/-18°C to 10°F/-12°C
	Zone 8	10°F/-12°C to 20°F/-7°C
	Zone 9	20°F/-7°C to 30°F/-1°C
	Zone 10	30°F/-1°C to 40°F/4°C
	Zone 11	Above 40°F/4°C

determine the zone where your garden is located.

The encyclopedia is divided into the major types of water plants with sections on floaters, oxygenators, water lilies, marginals, and bog plants, as well as moisture-loving trees and shrubs. Read the information provided with each plant for its specific needs, but don't shy away from experimenting with a particular species by placing it in less-than-ideal conditions. Plants are surprisingly adaptable.

You don't need to limit your choice of plants to those in this encyclopedia. They are some of the most prominent and popular varieties and can form the backbone of your garden, but they represent just a fraction of what's available.

See the list of suppliers on page 186.

TIPS ON PURCHASING PLANTS

Thanks to the recent boom in water gardening, finding plants for a pond is far easier than it once was. Nowadays, even general garden centers often sell plants suitable for a water or bog garden. But for a greater selection—including the more rare varieties—you should do the majority of your shopping through companies that specialize in water gardening. Don't worry if there isn't one in your area. Most of these firms do much of their business through the mail. See the list of suppliers on page 186.

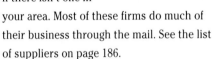

During the planning process, contact suppliers to find out what they have in stock and at what cost. This will allow you time to consider what is feasible for your garden as you are designing it. If you are having the plants shipped by mail, order them as early as possible, sometime between October and April—water gardening suppliers are invariably extremely busy during the growing season.

Normally, you will be given some choice as to when you want the plants delivered. It is best to get the plants in the garden as soon as you can, so have them delivered when you think you'll be putting in the garden. If this is your first attempt at water gardening, you might consider purchasing one of the collections offered by some suppliers. These typically include all the plants you will need for a well-balanced pool.

Before you place any mail order, ask the dealer about the age and size of the plants you will be receiving. As they sometimes have to travel great distances, plants may arrive damaged. Make certain the supplier will replace them free of charge. Also inquire how they will be delivered. Some suppliers ship plants in tiny plastic containers, which helps ensure they are kept damp, but the added weight can increase shipping costs substantially. Plants shipped with their roots bare are lighter and, therefore, more economical, but they must be handled with great care to avoid damage.

When the plants arrive, unpack them in a shady location and place them in the pool. Do not remove the protective wrapping until you are ready to plant. If you won't be planting for several days or more, plant them in pots and store them in a warm, lighted place. Before you put them in the garden, identify each one with a permanent plastic label.

WATER LILIES *(HARDY CULTIVARS)*

HARDY CULTIVARS
Nymphaea spp. (water lilies)

Plant from 16"-24" deep in calm water. Prefer sun. Can overwinter if rhizome remains below ice level. Control vigorous species in artificial ponds by planting in baskets. Leaves are heart- or oval-shaped, each attached to the rhizome by its own stem. Flowers come out between May and October and float on the surface of the water.
Propagation: Root cuttings; separate shoots on the rhizome.
Zones: 5-10

Alba
Description: *White blooms with yellow centers.*
Spread: *3 sq. ft.*

Attraction
Description: *Garnet red flowers.*
Spread: *4-8 sq. ft.*

Chromatella
Description: *Canary yellow flowers.*
Spread: *1-8 sq. ft.*

Gladstoniana
Description: *Pure white, waxy flowers with broad petals and yellow centers.*
Spread: *4-8 sq. ft.*

Odorata
Description: *Sulfur-yellow star-shaped flowers.*
Spread: *4-12 sq. ft.*

Pink Sensation
Description: *Deep pink flowers with cream-colored edges.*
Spread: *3-6 sq. ft.*

Pygmaea helvola
Description: *Light yellow blooms with darker centers.*
Spread: *2 sq. ft.*

Sultan
Description: *Pink blossom changes to cherry red on second day.*
Spread: *6-12 sq. ft.*

TROPICAL CULTIVARS
Nymphaea spp. (water lilies)

Plant in 8"-12" of soil 4"-12" deep in shallow water.

Prefer sun. Water temperature must not go below 41°F. Remove tubers from outdoor pool before first frost and store in frost-free environment.

Propagation: Seed; separate eyes that develop on the tuber.

Zones: 10, 11

Albert Greenberg
Description: *Day bloomer. Cup-shaped flowers blend orange, yellow, and dark pink. Foliage mottled.*
Spread: *6-10 sq. ft.*

August Koch
Description: *Day bloomer. Light purple blooms with golden centers.*
Spread: *4-8 sq. ft.*

Evelyn Randig
Description: *Day bloomer. Magenta star-shaped flower with yellow center. Foliage variegated with magenta and chestnut.*
Spread: *6-8 sq. ft.*

General Pershing
Description: *Bright pink blooms open in morning and close at dusk.*
Spread: *6-12 sq. ft.*

Daubeniana
Description: *Day bloomer. Small lavender-blue flowers.*
Spread: *1-3 sq. ft.*

Pink Perfection
Description: *Day bloomer. Lavender-pink blossoms. Mottled foliage.*
Spread: *6-8 sq. ft.*

Red Flare
Description: *Night bloomer. Dusky red, star-like flower with long, narrow petals. Deep mahogany-red foliage.*
Spread: *6-8 sq. ft.*

Nelumbo spp. (lotus)
Description: *Rounded leaves that can reach a width of up to 2'. Flowers from June to October; blooms can be as much as 12" wide.*
Spread: *12 sq. ft.*

Texas Shell Pink
Description: *Night bloomer. Huge star-shaped, pale pink blossoms.*
Spread: *6-8 sq. ft.*

Yellow Dazzler
Description: *Day bloomer. Bright yellow, double blossoms. Speckled foliage.*
Spread: *6-10 sq. ft.*

FLOATING PLANTS

Eichhornia crassipes (water hyacinth)
Floats in any depth. Prefers hot, sunny position.
Height: 8" above water surface.
Description: Shiny, rounded leaves grow in a rosette. Sprays of pale lavender-blue flowers appear from June-September.
Propagation: Throws out runners.
Zone: 10

Pistia stratiotes (water lettuce)
Floats in water 4"-6" deep. Prefers hot, sunny position in calm, shallow water.
Height: 2"-4" above water surface.
Description: Velvety green leaves grow in rosettes from June till October.
Propagation: By seeds; separate lateral shoots that have produced roots.
Zones: 8-10

Salvinia rotundifolia (water fern)
Floats on surface of water. Prefers hot, sunny position. Helps to control algae. Remove with a net if it becomes invasive.
Description: Small leaves covered with tiny hairs absorb nutrients from the water.
Propagation: Separate plants in summer.
Zone: 10

OXYGENATING PLANTS

Cabomba spp.
Plant in coarse, sandy soil, 2" deep, submerged under 12" of water. Prefers sunny location.
Description: Leaves vary depending on species.
Propagation: By root division.
Zones: 5-10, depending on species.

Elodea canadensis (Canadian pondweed)
Weight plant with a small stone and drop into water 1'-5' deep, up to 5 plants per sq. yd. Prefers sunny conditions but will tolerate shade. If growth becomes too vigorous, remove excess with a rake.
Description: Tiny, dark green, lance-shaped leaves on threadlike branches.
Propagation: By stem cuttings.
Zones: 5-10

Potamogeton spp. (pondweeds)
Plant in water from 8"-10" deep, up to 5 plants per sq. yd. Prefers a sunny position.
Description: Wavy-edged, bronze-green foliage. Flowers appear between June and August.
Propagation: By stem cuttings.
Zones: 5-10

Vallisneria americana (eelgrass)
Plant in sandy slightly acid soil submerged under water 6"-24" deep.
Description: Slender ribbonlike leaves that float beneath the water surface.
Propagation: Division of runners.
Zone: 9

**Aponogeton distachyus
(water hawthorn)**
Plant in water 2"-3" deep. Prefers semishade.
If winters are severe—below -4°F—plant in
baskets which can be taken out of water.
Height: 1'-3'.
Description: Green leaves float on surface
of water. White flowers appear year round.
Propagation: Seeds germinate readily, even
while still on plant. Division of rhizomes,
separation of lateral shoots.
Zones: 9-10

Caltha palustris (marsh marigold)
Plant March to April in rich, damp soil or
in water up to 8" deep, 6-8 plants per sq.
yd. Prefers rich, wet soil and sun. Hardy
perennial common throughout the cold
and temperate regions of North America.
Height: 8"-20".
Spread: 12".
Description: Heart-shaped dark-green
dentate leaves. Numerous bright golden-
yellow flowers from March-April.
Propagation: By seed or divide roots during the growing season.
Zones: 6-10

Carex spp. (sedges)
Plant between October and April in moist soil.
Prefers wet, peaty soils. Likes hot sunny areas
but will tolerate semishade.
Height: 6"-5' depending on species.
Description: Stiff, sharp-edged leaves grow
from the base of a solid, nodeless stem.
Brownish flower spikes from May to
September.
Propagation: By seeds or divide clumps in
spring.
Zones: 6-10

**Canna hybrids: 'Ra,' 'Erebus,'
'Endeavor' (canna)**
Plant in early June in damp soil with
lots of rotted manure or under up to
8" of water. Prefers rich, wet soil and
lots of sun. Apply fertilizer or manure
throughout growing period. In
autumn, dry tubers and store at
41°-50° F.
Height: 3'-7'.
Description: Large, pointed green
leaves. Large flowers from June to
October.
Propagation: Divide plants after
flowering.
Zones: 9-10

**Crinum americanum
(Florida swamp lily)**
Plant in rich soil submerged in up to 12" of
water. Prefers sunny location. Shelter from
wind. Sensitive to transplantation.
Description: Long narrow leaves that grow up
to 2" wide. White flowers may be tinged green
or purple.
Propagation: Divide tubers in summer.
Zones: 9-11

**Cyperus alternifolius
(umbrella grass)**
Plant in shallow water. Prefers
a sunny location.
Height: 3'3".
Spread: 3'.
Description: Tall stems topped
with an umbrella of leaves.
Propagation: Division of roots.
Zones: 9-10

MARGINAL/BOG PLANTS

**Cyperus papyrus
(Nile grass)**
*Plant in shallow water. Prefers
a sunny location.*
Height: *8'-12'.*
Spread: *10'-13'.*
Description: *Triangular stems
topped with long, needlelike
leaves in a pompon.*
Propagation: *Division of
rhizomes.*
Zone: *8*

**Eleocharis spp.
(Chinese water chestnut)**
*Plant submerged in water up to 6" deep. Prefers slightly
acid soil in sunny or semishaded situation.*
Height: *1'-3'.*
Description: *Tubular green jointed stems. Occasionally
produces flower spikelets on the end of a stem.*
Propagation: *Roots produce bulbs (corms), which can be
removed and replanted.*
Zones: *7-10*

Equisetum spp. (horsetails)
*Plant in wet soil or in water up to 6" deep.
Plant in containers or use an effective root bar-
rier; stolons spread rapidly and are difficult to
control. Prefers sun or semishade.*
Height: *6"-3' depending on species.*
Spread: *Unlimited; keep contained.*
Description: *Dark green hollow stems with
dark bands at nodes.*
Propagation: *Division of stolons.*
Zones: *4-10*

**Houttuynia cordata
'Chameleon'**
*Plant in damp soil or in water up to
12" deep, 6 plants per sq. yd.
Vigorous easy-to-grow plant adapts
well to any growing situation.*
Height: *6"-12".*
Spread: *12".*
Description: *Cultivar with variegat-
ed foliage, purplish green, yellow,
bronze, and red. Best in autumn.*
Propagation: *Division of established
plants in spring or autumn.*
Zone: *6*

**Hydrocleys nymphoides
(water poppy)**
*Plant in water 8"-24" deep. Prefers
sunny position. Overwinter in pool
or damp soil in greenhouse.*
Height: *4".*
Description: *Shiny, heart-shaped,
dark green leaves with yellow
flowers from May to October.*
Propagation: *Divide crown in
spring.*
Zone: *10*

Iris pseudacorus (yellow flag)
*Plant in damp soil or in water up to
1' deep. A vigorous easy-to-grow
plant that will tolerate alkaline soil.
Prefers a boggy, sunny situation.*
Height: *3'3"-5'.*
Spread: *20".*
Description: *Light-green, broad,
sword-shaped leaves and bright
yellow flowers that bloom from
June to July.*
Propagation: *Sow seed in spring
and early summer or divide clumps
after flowering.*
Zones: *4-10*

Iris ensata (Japanese iris)
*Plant from September to the end
of March in damp soil or in water
up to 4" deep. Prefers moist, acid
soil and sun or semishade.*
Height: *36".*
Spread: *18".*
Description: *Slender deciduous
foliage and purple flowers from
early June to late July. Many cultivars have white, pink, lavender,
wine combinations of colors.*
Propagation: *Division of clumps
every 4 years.*
Zones: *5-10*

Iris sibirica (Siberian iris)
Plant in damp soil 2" deep. A hardy plant for water gardens that can adapt to drier conditions. Prefers sun or semi-shade, neutral to acid soil.
Height: 3'3".
Spread: 3'3".
Description: Erect narrow leaves. Flowers range from blue to white and bloom from late spring to early summer.
Propagation: By seed or divide clumps every 5 years.
Zones: 4-10

Iris versicolor
(blue flag, wild iris)
Plant 2"-4" deep.
Height: 2'-2¹/₂'.
Description: Sword-shaped medium-green leaves. Violet-blue flowers have a yellow patch and appear in the early summer. Smaller North American version of the Iris pseudacorus.
Propagation: By seed or root division after flowering.
Zones: 4-10

Juncus spiralis effusus (corkscrew rush)
Plant close together in wet soil or in water up to 8" deep. Hardy plants with creeping roots that help stabilize pond margins. Prefers sun or semishade.
Height: 12"-20" or 13'-16'.
Description: Dark-green leaves shaped like a corkscrew.
Propagation: By division in early spring.
Zones: 5-10

Lobelia cardinalis (cardinal flower)
Plant in moist soil or in water up to 6" deep, 5-6 plants per sq. yd. Prefers sun but will tolerate shade. Needs protection in winter.
Height: 4"-20".
Description: Green foliage with bright red flowers from July to October.
Propagation: By seed or division of clumps in spring.
Zones: 7-10

Ludwigia spp.
Plant in water 12"-20" deep, 5 plants per sq. yd. Prefers sunny position. Control by cutting back its stems throughout the growing season.
Height: Stalks up to 16' long rising 4" above water.
Description: Bright yellow blooms from June through September.
Propagation: Terminal and lateral stem cuttings carrying adventitious roots.
Zone: 10

Marsilea mutica (water clover)
Plant in water up to 1' deep. Prefers sunny location.
Description: Flowerless. Leaves are two shades of glossy green.
Propagation: Spores, division.
Zones: 9-10

Menyanthes trifoliata (marsh trefoil)
Plant in very wet soil or in water up to 12" deep, 5-10 plants per sq. yd. Hardy perennial with a creeping root that either floats or is anchored to the bottom.
Height: 6"-12" above water level.
Description: Clusters of star-shaped fringed white flowers bloom from April to June.
Propagation: By seed or division of rhizome in spring.
Zones: 6-10

Mimulus cardinalis (monkey flower)
Plant in wet soil or in water up to 8". Hardy perennial that self-seeds easily.
Height: 24"-30".
Description: Flowers ranging from yellow to red bloom from July through September.
Propagation: Seeds in spring or divide the crown.
Zones: 8-10

MARGINAL/BOG PLANTS

**Myosotis scorpiodes
(water forget-me-not)**
*Plant in damp soil or in water up to 6" deep,
20 plants per sq. yd. Good in sun or shade.
Height: 8"-16" (above soil).
Description: Sky-blue flowers bloom from
May through October.
Propagation: Division of clumps in spring,
seed in autumn.
Zones: 5-10*

**Myriophyllum aquaticum
(parrot's feather)**
*Plant in water 3"-12" deep. Likes full sun but
will grow in semishaded location. Must be far
below ice to survive over-freezing in winter.
Description: Pink stems with striking green
foliage. Tops of plants emerge from water.
Propagation: Remove shoots in spring and
plant in ground.
Zone: 10*

Nymphoides indica (water snowflake)
*Plant submerged in 1'-3' of water.
Prefers full sun.
Description: Glossy pale green heart-shaped
leaves. White flowers with fringed petals
and yellow centers float just above the water
surface.
Propagation: By seed, division in spring,
separation of plantlets in autumn.
Zone: 10*

Nymphoides peltata (fringed water lily)
*Plant under 1'-2½' of water, 5 plants per sq.
yd. Prefers sun or semishade. Cultivate in
containers to prevent it taking all available
space.
Height: 2"-4" above water.
Description: Heart-shaped leaves float on
water. Yellow flowers bloom from July to October.
Propagation: By seed, root cuttings in spring.
Zones: 6-10*

Orontium aquaticum (golden club)
*Plant up to 16" deep, 5 plants per sq. yd.
Hardy, slow-growing perennial prefers sun or
semishade.
Height: 18" above water level
Description: Large, blue-green, spear-shaped
leaves. Flowers are white stalks with erect yel-
low spadices that appear in March.
Propagation: By seed or root cutting that con-
tains a node.
Zones: 8-10*

Peltandra virginica (arrow arum)
*Plant 3" deep. Hardy plant with roots that
travel almost 3' into the soil.
Height: 1½'-2'.
Description: Dark-green, glossy, arrowhead-
like foliage with greenish white flowers that
bloom in summer.
Propagation: Division in early spring.
Zones: 7-10*

**Pontederia cordata
(pickerel weed)**
*Plant in rich soil under water
6"-16" deep. Prefers sun or
semishade. Protect crown
against frost.
Height: 16"-26".
Description: Spear-shaped
leaves and spikes of blue
flowers that bloom from June
through August.
Propagation: Divide roots
in spring.
Zones: 9-10*

**Sagittaria latifolia
(arrowhead or broad-
leaved arrowhead)**
*Plant under 2"-12" of water.
Prefers sun or semishade and
needs shelter in winter.
Height: 16"-24".
Description: Broad, arrow-
shaped leaves with pure white
flowers that bloom from June
to August.
Propagation: Divide clumps
of plants in the summer and
separate the tubercles in
winter and early spring.
Zones: 7-10*

Sagittaria japonica (Japanese arrowhead)

Plant under no more than 5" of water. Prefers sun or semishade.
Height: *12"-30".*
Spread: *8".*
Description: *Broad, arrow-shaped leaves with double white flowers that bloom from June to August.*
Propagation: *Divide clumps of plants in the summer and separate the tubercles in winter and early spring.*
Zones: *7-10*

Saururus cernuus (lizard's-tail)

Plant in damp soil or in water up to 16" deep. This hardy perennial prefers sun and semishade.
Height: *2'-4'.*
Spread: *5'.*
Description: *Olive green, heart-shaped leaves that turn crimson in autumn with tiny creamy white flowers that bloom from June to August.*
Propagation: *Divide clumps in spring or separate offshoots.*
Zones: *5-10*

Typha angustifolia (narrow-leaved cattail)

Plant in rich soil between May and October. Prefers a hot, sunny position. This hardy perennial is best cultivated in tubs as it is very invasive.
Height: *5'-7'.*
Spread: *3'.*
Description: *Narrow light green foliage with reddish-brown flower heads that appear between June and August.*
Propagation: *Divide the rhizome in spring.*
Zones: *3-10*

Typha latifolia (reed mace, false bulrush, cattail)

Plant in rich soil between May and October. Prefers a hot, sunny position. This vigorous perennial is best cultivated in large pools.
Height: *7'-10'.*
Spread: *3'.*
Description: *Narrow gray-green foliage with dark brown flower heads that appear between June and August.*
Propagation: *Divide the rhizome in spring.*
Zones: *4-10*

Thalia dealbata (water canna)

Plant in rich soil in water 8"-24" deep. In a continental climate, winter shelter is required to protect the crown from freezing.
Height: *3'-5'.*
Description: *Blue-green, spear-shaped leaves, long stems with spikes of dark blue flowers that bloom from June to September.*
Propagation: *Root division, separate suckers in the spring. This subtropical perennial prefers a hot, sunny position.*
Zones: *9-10*

Scirpus spp. (bulrushes)

Plant 3"-5" deep in rich soil in up to 6" of water.
Height: *12"*
Description: *Grasslike leaves with round flowers located at tips of stems.*
Propagation: *By seed, division of rootstock.*
Zones: *8-10*

Zantedeschia aethiopica (calla lily)

Plant in very damp soil or in water up to 12" deep. Prefers full sun or semishade. Protect the crown in winter. In extreme climates, winter in a greenhouse.
Height: *36".*
Spread: *36".*
Description: *Heart-shaped dark green leaves with white flowers shaped like open horns that bloom throughout the spring and summer.*
Propagation: *Divide the rhizome during the dormant period or remove suckers.*
Zones: *8-10*

MOISTURE-LOVING PLANTS

Adiantum pedatum (maidenhair fern)
Plant in damp, humus-rich soil. Prefers semishade.
Height: 20".
Description: Bright green, fan-shaped leaflets on thin, dark stems.
Propagation: Division of the plant or from spores.
Zones: 8-10

Astilbe spp.
Plant in damp soil in early autumn, 6-8 plants per sq. yd. Prefers shade or semishade but can tolerate sun if roots are kept damp.
Height: 6"-78"depending on variety.
Description: The various species of this plant produce feathery panicles of flowers in many shades, including white, pink, violet, carmine, bronze. Blooms appear from May to September.
Propagation: Division in spring or autumn.
Zones: 5-6

Bamboo
Plant in moist, cool soil under 4" of mulch to protect from drying out. Young plants prefer shade. Some varieties require sun for best color, others prefer shade. Use barriers around the plants to control their invasive root system.
Height: 8"-115' depending on climate and species.
Description: There are more than 1,000 species of this perennial grass, some are evergreen and others deciduous. They rarely flower.
Propagation: Division of clumps.
Zones: 6-10

Betula pendula Youngii (Young's weeping birch)
Tolerates any soil and situation.
Height: 12'.
Spread: 10'.
Description: Graceful, pendulous branches; silver-white bark.
Propagation: By seed, grafting.
Zones: 4-5

Glyceria aquatica
Plant in wet soil or submerged to 20", 10 plants per sq. yd. A hardy perennial with a creeping root system that helps stabilize pond margins.
Height: 5'-8'.
Description: Luminous green foliage from May to November. Flowers June to August.
Propagation: By seed, division of clump.
Zone: 6

Hemerocallis cultivars (daylily)
Plant in deep, nutrient-rich, moist or dry soil or submerged in water 2"-4" deep, 5 plants per sq. yd. Prefers sun or semishade.
Height: 24"-30".
Description: Foliage from early spring to late autumn. Flowers appear from May to September and come in a wide range of shades depending on the species.
Propagation: Divide clumps in autumn.
Zones: 5-10

Hosta cultivars
Plant in wet or damp acidic soil, 16" apart.
Prefers sun or semisun but can tolerate shade
if soil is moist.
Height: 12"-24" with flowers reaching 24"-30".
Description: Foliage ranges from yellow-green
to blue-green. Some cultivars have white
variegations. White, blue, or lilac flowers
appear from May to September.
Propagation: Divide crown in spring.
Zones: 5-10

Ligularia spp.
Plant in moist soil, 3-4 plants per sq. yd. Prefers
sun and semishade. Shelter from wind.
Height: 3'-5'.
Spread: 3'.
Description: Shape of the leaves varies with
the species. Flowers, of various colors depend-
ing on the species, bloom between July and
September.
Propagation: By seed, division of clumps in
spring.
Zones: 6-8

Liriope spp. (lilyturfs)
Plant in well-drained, sandy soil. Prefers sun or
semishade.
Height: 12"-20".
Description: Dark green, glossy leaves.
Depending on the species, flowers range from
bluish lilac to white and appear from late sum-
mer to the end of autumn.
Propagation: Division of rhizomes in spring.
Zones: 9-10

**Matteuccia struthiopteris
(ostrich fern)**
Plant in groups in rich soil next to
pond.
Height: 36".
Spread: 18".
Description: Curving foliage
resembles ostrich feathers.
Propagation: By spores.
Zones: 9-10

**Phalaris arundinacea
(ribbon grass, lady's garters)**
Plant in damp soil or submerged to 14", 10-20
plants per sq. yd. This hardy perennial prefers a
sunny position. It also tolerates dry ground.
Height: 3'-5'.
Description: Ribbonlike foliage from May to
November. Violet flowers appear from June to
July.
Propagation: By seed, division of crowns.
Zones: 4-10

Primula spp. (primroses)
Plant in damp, acid soil. These hardy perennials
prefer semishade.
Height: 16", Flowers can reach 3'.
Spread: 3'.
Description: Broad, pale green crinkled
leaves. Flowers appear from April to June.
Colors range from blue to pink to crimson.
Propagation: Division of clumps after
flowering.
Zones: 5-10

Spartina pectinata (prairie cordgrass)
Plant in wet or damp soil. Prefers sunny
position. Helpful in stabilizing pond margins.
Height: 5'-7'.
Spread: 3'.
Description: Long ribbonlike foliage from June
through November. Brown inflorescence in
September.
Propagation: By seed, division of rootstock.
Zones: 5-10

Pond
Inhabitants
AND GUESTS

While plants and flowers provide the majority of color and diversity in a water garden, often it's fish and other forms of wildlife that make it a truly natural setting. Adding goldfish or koi to the pool, for example, creates an aquatic habitat that is well balanced in both animal and plant life. This chapter will provide information on how to introduce fish to the pond and care for them once they're in place. As well as fish, there are many other creatures—from birds to frogs to turtles—that can find a comfortable home in and around your garden pond. You'll find information on these and others on the following pages. The encyclopedia section toward the end of the chapter offers photos and descriptions of a variety of pond inhabitants.

If there are any creatures common to water garden settings, koi and goldfish fit the bill. Living happily together, they bring color and movement to any pool. It's always best to keep the water as clear as possible to appreciate their beauty.

Pond Fish

Sooner or later, you'll probably be tempted to include fish in your garden pond. The most common choices traditionally have been goldfish and koi, because of their bright colors and their easy-going habits. But other options range from a few minnows for a tub garden to a whole school of trout for a large pond. Whatever species you decide on, the basic requirements for healthy fish are pretty much the same. The following pages offer a brief look at fish biology and outline the types of fish common to garden pools.

BASIC FISH BIOLOGY

Basic fish biology does not change much from species to species. Listed here, and illustrated below and on the opposite page, are the main physical features and characteristics of fish.

Breathing: Water passes through the fish's mouth and over the gills, the fish equivalent of lungs. Fine blood vessels in the gills absorb the oxygen into the bloodstream directly from the water. Veins going to and from the gills take oxygenated blood to the heart, and bring back the deoxygenated blood, including such gases as carbon dioxide, to be released. Although gill covers protect the gills, it is still important that the water be clean to avoid infection.

Mouth shape: Different species of fish have different feeding habits. There are bottom feeders, mid-water feeders, and surface feed-

OUTSIDE THE FISH

A fish's sensory organs—eyes, nostrils, mouth, lateral line, and possibly barbels—allow it to perceive and locate both food and dangers in its environment. Its various fins work together to move it through the water, allow it to stop, and to hover.

Nostrils
Sensors inside allow fish to perceive odors.

Eyes
Provide good vision, but can't both focus on same object. Very sensitive to infection.

Mouth
Inferior position indicates fish is bottom feeder.

Dorsal fin
Extends from the highest point of the back toward the tail. How far back it extends depends on the species of fish. Keeps the fish from rolling over, and can be lowered for faster motion.

Caudal peduncle
Muscles in the area just in front of the tail fin control its motion.

Gill covers
Also called opercula (singular: operculum); protect gills.

Barbels
Common on bottom-feeding fish, they allow the fish to sense food even in debris-clouded water.

Pectoral fins
Help the fish to make rapid turns and act as brakes.

Ventral fins
Direct the fish's movements side to side or up and down.

Anal fin
Helps keep the fish stable.

Tail (or caudal) fin
Moves the fish through water. Generally, faster-moving fish have a more deeply forked tail fin than slower-moving fish.

ers. The position of the mouth is a good indication of where the fish gets its food: A bottom feeder will have a turned down (inferior) mouth; a surface feeder's mouth will be turned up (superior), and a mid-water feeder's mouth will be more or less horizontal (terminal).
Hearing: Fish's ears pick up even minor sound vibrations in the water. They don't need the external projections that human ears have to amplify sound because water is a good conductor of sound.
Lateral line: Fish have lines of specialized cells on each side of their body that detect changes in water current. Hairs in the cells collect this information, which nerves then send to the brain. Depending on the species, the cells may be in one line extending partway or all the way from head to tail, or several lines, or distributed over the body.
Scales: Fish scales, formed in the lower layer of the skin, are transparent, which allows pigments deeper in the skin to show through and give the fish its characteristic color and scale type. A fish's scales continue to grow throughout its lifetime, so it is possible to get a rough idea of the age of a given fish by examining its scales.

Fish are covered with a transparent slime coating, which helps protect them from bacterial infection and also makes them feel slippery. If you must touch a fish, wet your hands first so as not to remove this coating and render the fish vulnerable to infection.

KOI

The first koi (called *nishikigoi* in Japanese) were developed centuries ago from carp *(Cyprinus carpio)* that were being raised for

Choosing koi of different types will create a pleasing palette of colors in your garden pool.

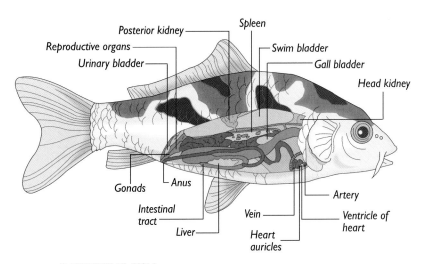

Posterior kidney — Spleen — Swim bladder — Gall bladder — Head kidney — Reproductive organs — Urinary bladder — Gonads — Anus — Intestinal tract — Liver — Heart auricles — Vein — Artery — Ventricle of heart

INSIDE THE FISH

Fish have essentially the same internal organs we do. One significant exception is the swim bladder, or air bladder, a hydrostatic organ derived from the digestive tract, that allows the fish to maintain its position in the water. Fish can regulate their position by adding or extracting gases, such as oxygen, from the swim bladder.

food. Around the turn of this century, most of the numerous color and pattern combinations that are recognized today were developed.

Differentiated by color, pattern, and scale type into 13 varieties, koi can be divided into single-color, two-color, three-color, and multi-color categories. Scales are classified as normal (like any other fish), metallic, or Doitsu, which means German in Japanese. This scale type was developed by crossing with a German carp. A pinecone pattern to the scales is called Matsuba, and koi that have extremely reflective scales are called Gin Rin or Kin Rin. Even metallic-scaled koi can have this type of scale.

The three most popular types are sometimes referred to as the "big three." These are: Kohaku (ko-ha-ku), a white fish with a red pattern; Taisho Sanke (tie-show-san-kay), a white fish with a red and black pattern; and Showa Sanke (showa-san-kay), a black fish with a red and white pattern. These and other varieties are shown in the encyclopedia beginning on page 120.

Japanese names for koi types often relate to the characteristic color patterns. For example, ki (kee) yellow, shiro (sherow) white, and hi (hee) or aka (a-ka) red, may be added to the type name to differentiate. Utsuri (oots-oo-ree) is a term for a fish with colored marking, either red, white, or yellow, on a black body. Ki Utsuri have yellow markings, Shiro Utsuri have white markings, and Hi Utsuri have red markings. Of course, you don't have to understand the nomenclature to choose a fish. Just select one that appeals to you and point it out to the dealer.

Koi can grow up to about 3 feet in length and may live for 50 or 60 years, perhaps longer. They are gregarious fish, and fairly easy to train. Some allow themselves to be petted and will even follow their owners around the pond.

Prize specimens can be very expensive, but young, small koi go for around $10. It's best to start with inexpensive fish until you gain some experience. Consider joining a koi club where enthusiasts are usually willing to offer help and advice.

GOLDFISH

Also from the carp family, goldfish (*Carassius auratus*) have been bred for centuries as hobby fish. They're a good choice for a pond because they're available in many varieties, they tolerate fluctuations in water temperature reasonably well, and will survive in water that's less than clean. They're normally quite docile, and can be mixed with other pond fish.

Good choices for outdoor ponds include the Common, Comet, and Shubunkin varieties. Other possibilities include the slightly more exotic Veiltail, Fantail, and Moor, all of which have more delicate finnage that may become a bit ragged in a pond. The very exotic types, such as the Bubble-eye, which has delicate enlarged sacs around its eyes, or the Lionhead, with its "raspberry-like" head growth and lack of dorsal fin, are not well suited to ponds—they need a stable water temperature, free from fluctuations.

Unlike koi, the size that goldfish attain depends to some extent on the size of their "home." In an outdoor pond, some species may reach lengths of up to 10 or 12 inches. Typical life span is about 3 to 4 years; 6 to 12 years is considered a long life.

OTHER FISH

Another good choice for a garden pond is the Golden Orfe (*Leuciscus idus*), a fast-swimming, bottom-feeding scavenger that grows to about 12 inches in length. It's a pretty, golden-colored fish that's imported from Europe, and can share a pond with goldfish or koi.

If you don't want your koi or goldfish to reproduce, some experts recommend keeping one sunfish (*Lepomis macrochirus*) as a biological control—it will eat the other fish eggs and fry.

For a small container garden, consider adding a couple of minnows (family *Cyprinidae*) or mosquito fish (*Gambusia affinis*), to help control bugs.

In a more naturalistic pond, you might want a school of darters (genera *Percina*, *Ammocrypta*, *Etheostoma*), or a few sticklebacks (family *Gasterosteidae*) or killifish (family *Cyprinodontidae*). For a large pond, you can consider stocking game fish, such as trout or catfish, but they're banned in some areas, so be sure to check with the Department of Fish and Game.

Goldfish of different types, including the flamboyant Fantail shown in the middle of the photo at left, help to create a diverse mix in the garden pool.

Bunched together near the surface of the water, a medium-size school of goldfish provides a vibrant accent to the rich greenery of this natural pond setting.

Fish Care

An established pond is relatively easy to take care of, but getting your pond to that state can be tricky. Requirements for a fish pond are briefly outlined on page 26; they're discussed in more detail on these pages, showing you how to establish a well-balanced pond for healthy fish.

Designing the fish pond: The shape of your pond is mostly a matter of preference, but adequate depth, especially for koi, is crucial. It must be no shallower than 18 inches, and depths of more than 24 inches are preferred. Deeper water also offers a refuge from predators. The pond must also be large enough so the fish have room to swim. Figure on 1,000 gallons as the minimum for a koi pond; that translates into a pool that is roughly 10 feet long by 8 feet wide by 20 inches deep. To calculate your pool's volume, see the formula on page 158. Goldfish can generally survive happily in smaller spaces.

The Nitrogen Cycle

Ammonia, a component of nitrogen, is toxic to fish and must be removed from the water. In a well-balanced natural aquatic environment, bacteria in the water break down ammonia into forms that plants and algae can consume. Fish then eat the plants and algae, producing more wastes that must be broken down. This process is called the "nitrogen cycle."

You can mimic this balance in the artificial environment of your pond by passing the water through a biological filter containing the necessary bacteria. Water flow through the filter must be constant to keep the bacteria alive.

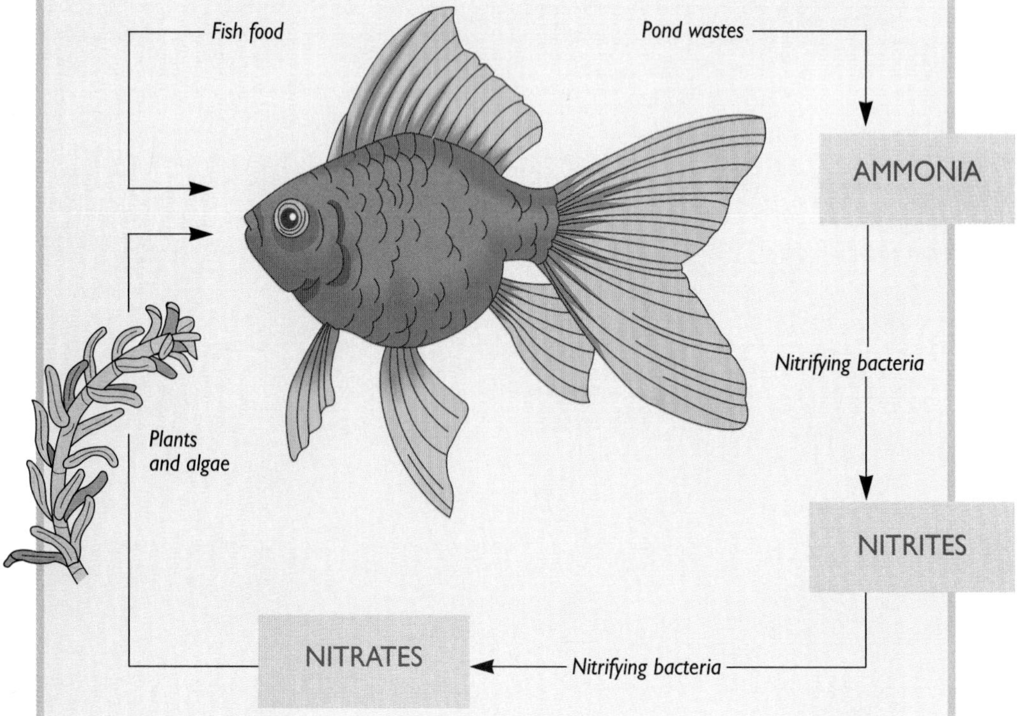

Fish food

Pond wastes

AMMONIA

Nitrifying bacteria

NITRITES

Plants and algae

NITRATES — Nitrifying bacteria

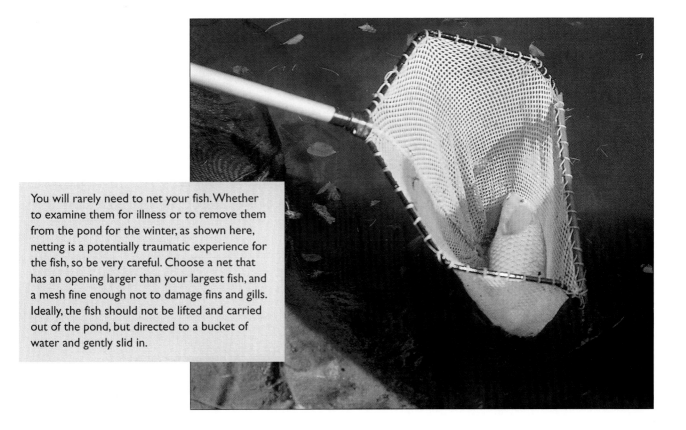

You will rarely need to net your fish. Whether to examine them for illness or to remove them from the pond for the winter, as shown here, netting is a potentially traumatic experience for the fish, so be very careful. Choose a net that has an opening larger than your largest fish, and a mesh fine enough not to damage fins and gills. Ideally, the fish should not be lifted and carried out of the pond, but directed to a bucket of water and gently slid in.

Pond depth depends to some extent on climate. If you live in a cold climate and plan to keep your fish outside all winter, you'll need to keep the water from freezing solid. A depth of about $2^1/2$ feet should suffice if you keep the water moving. If the water is still, use a pond heater.

If your pool is for fish only, place it where it gets some shade. This is good for the fish—their colors tend to be richer and deeper in shade—and it will keep down algae formation. Floating plants, such as water lettuce and water hyacinth, and plants with floating leaves, such as lilies, can also provide shade for fish. Surface exchange of gases, such as carbon dioxide, is important, so don't cover more than half of the surface with plant material.

Fish, and especially koi, tend to forage in pots, so add a layer of rocks and gravel on top of the soil. Some experts recommend placing new plants in protective cages until they're established, or even designing a pond with a separate area for plants, protected from the fish by a rock dam.

If you really want to enjoy your colorful fish, pond water should be as clear as possible. A pool filter will keep the water clear; the best ponds often have a combination of biological and mechanical filters, such as a pressurized-sand filter. The biological filter is the workhorse; the pressurized-sand filter simply serves as a "polishing" filter. But it's possible, if the water is well balanced, to have a

crystal clear pool with no filter mechanism at all. This is most likely to occur in a pond with only a few fish.

Balancing the water: One of the most important aspects of fish care is creating a healthy aquatic home for them. The water must be well oxygenated, and must not contain harmful chemicals.

To ensure that your fish will get enough oxygen, the pond's surface area must be as great as possible; in addition, some aeration—in the form of a fountain, waterfall, or venturi *(page 60)*—is beneficial.

Toxic chemicals to look out for include ammonia, chlorine, and chloramines. Ammonia is produced by fish wastes and other wastes, such as uneaten food and plant debris on the pool bottom. The key to understanding ammonia buildup—and its eradication— lies in the nitrogen cycle *(page 106)*. In the presence of beneficial bacteria, ammonia is reduced to nitrites, which in turn break down into nitrates that can be taken up by plants and fish.

Biological filtration is one way to deal with ammonia; mechanical filtration with zeolite as the medium is also touted by some experts. Natural filtration from plants such as the water hyacinth can be very effective. You can monitor the ammonia situation in your pond with an ammonia test kit.

Other problems include chlorine and chloramines. Chlorine, which is added to most municipal water supplies, is bad for fish in large amounts; fortunately, it will dissipate in a few days if the water is left standing, faster if you circulate the water with a pump. Chloramines, combinations of chlorine and ammonia, may be added to your local water. They're very toxic to fish, and you'll have to take chemical steps to break them down. Consult a pond supply store.

The pH (acidity) levels are also important. The best pH for a fish pond is between 6.5 and 7.5. You can check the pH of the water with a pH testing kit.

Newly installed ponds tend to take a little time to find their balance—about a month or two. Most new ponds will go through a cloudy, green stage of high algae levels about two to three weeks after they're installed. Algae thrive on the nutrients in the fresh water, and in the abundant sunlight they receive before your potted plants have grown enough to give shade. Once

Your fish should eat ravenously when you feed them. As soon as they seem uninterested, stop feeding. Uneaten food simply fouls the water, making your filter work harder.

the plants get established, they'll compete with the algae for the nutrients and bring shade to the pool, essentially starving the algae out. Resist the temptation to treat the water with algicides, because they'll also stunt the growth of the plants necessary for maintaining proper balance in the long run.

Proprietary products for getting your pond water in shape are available from pet stores and various mail-order sources. But do be patient, and remember that you're creating a long-term environment for living organisms.

Complete water changes are not recommended, but once your pond is established, partial water changes, which dilute harmful chemicals, should be part of regular maintenance. For more details on balancing and maintaining your pond water see page 176.

Buying fish: For a new pond, it's best to start with only a few fish, adding one or two to their numbers slowly. You can introduce new fish to your collection once the filtering system is in top shape, the water is well aerated, and the fish you started with are healthy. For the beginner, it may be difficult to find a reputable dealer—ask an experienced friend or neighbor for a referral; for koi, try a local koi club for assistance.

Examine the fish in their tanks for a while before you buy. Healthy fish are active, even in summer weather. They should not be hanging listlessly in midwater, or at the bottom of the tank. Their fins should be held erect, not closed or folded in, and they should not be rubbing themselves against the bottom or sides, as if trying to scratch. This is a sign of parasites.

It's best to start with medium-sized fish; very young fish may not make the adjustment to your pond, and fully grown fish are usually quite expensive. Your new pond inhabitants will probably adapt better if you select a few, rather than a single specimen.

Introducing fish to the pond: Most fish are transported in a plastic bag containing a small amount of water and a lot of air. If they're traveling a long distance, a blast of pure oxygen will be added. When transferring your fish to the pool, don't just dump them in. Instead, float the bag on the surface for 15 to 20 minutes, so the water temperature in the bag gradually adjusts to that of the pond. If the day is warm and sunny, drape a towel over the bag to shade the fish. Next, open the bag and ease the fish into the pool. They'll probably take off and hide;

gradually, over a period of days—but sometimes weeks—they will begin to feed and come out more.

If you're introducing new fish into an established pond, some experts recommend that you place them in a quarantine pool, or separate tank, for up to three weeks. This will enable you to screen the fish for diseases; if a fish is sick, it can be treated before the entire pond is infected.

Feeding: The number one rule is this: Don't overfeed your fish. They can only eat a small amount at a time, and the rest can end up sinking to the bottom, where it rots and quickly fouls the water. Feed them the amount they will eat ravenously, and no more. Scoop any food that is uneaten out of the pond with a net. If you have a pond containing both fish and plants, you may not even need to feed your fish. If they're hungry, fish nibble at insects in the pool and on algae or fast-growing oxygenating plants.

Goldfish and koi are omnivorous: they'll eat almost anything. Packaged foods, containing a balance of protein, carbohydrates, and vitamins, are recommended; some koi foods contain spirulina (a high-protein algae) or carotene as "color enhancers." Floating foods won't foul the water; uneaten pellets can easily be netted and removed from the pond.

Diversity is healthy for fish. Basic rations can be supplemented with worms, daphnia, brine shrimp, and ant eggs. Choose frozen or dried forms of these treats, as they are less likely to carry disease

Fish digestion works faster in warmer water so it's best to feed them during the day, rather than at night. As winter approaches and the water temperature drops, fish appetites gradually decrease. You should feed them progressively less as the water temperature drops. At about 45°, koi effectively begin to hibernate, living off

body fat until spring when warmer water rouses them from their dormant period. In the spring, reverse the process, gradually feeding them more as the water begins to warm up and their activity level increases accordingly.

Breeding fish: Your fish will probably breed of their own accord, but you might not want to allow their numbers to increase substantially, since that could upset the balance of the water and plant life in the pond. Depending on the style of pond you have, there's a good chance that none of the fry will reach maturity. In fact, many fish eat their own eggs and those of other species; other pond creatures also feed on fish eggs. A good biological control of fish reproduction is to stock one sunfish, also called a bluegill (*Lepomis sp.*), which will eat all the fish eggs and fry likely to be produced in a garden pond.

On the other hand, if you want to improve the chances of suc-

---

TRAINING KOI

Friendly, outgoing fish, koi can be trained to eat from their owner's hand. In a natural pond, feeding them is often not necessary as they will live off of the existing plants and algae, but it is a pleasurable experience. As well, seeing each of your fish daily gives you the opportunity to monitor their health, so you'll probably notice any diseases or parasites sooner. Training is usually easier with larger groups of fish, but even if you have only a few fish, it may be successful.

Begin by feeding them at the same time every day, usually in the morning, and at the same place. Then, stop feeding for a few days, but at feeding time slowly approach the pool. After two days, dangle your fingers in the water at the side of the pool. Do this for another two or three days. Finally, when you dangle your fingers in the water, leave a little food. The koi will have become used to your arrival, and will associate your appearance with food.

cessful fish reproduction, you can move spawning fish to a separate holding tank or blocked off area of the pond. Or add a commercially available spawning mop, designed to hold the fish eggs, to the pond. Once the fish have spawned, you can move it to a separate tank or area of the pond so the fry can develop safely.

Keep in mind that goldfish and koi do not breed true to their color patterns. You may also end up with a number of deformed or otherwise undesirable fish, so be prepared to do some significant culling of the fry to create the school of fish you want.

Once you've established your fish pond, you may find that your friends and neighbors aren't the only ones interested in the progress of your fish. Domestic explorers like the family cat or neighborhood hound, or wilder visitors such as raccoons, and even skunks, may drop by looking for a little fun or the proverbial free lunch. Birds such as kingfishers, egrets, and herons are a problem in some areas. Any one of these predators can devastate a prized fish collection in a very short time.

How do you ward them off? Sufficient pond depth, 24 inches or deeper, is a big help. Most mammals can't latch onto your fish while swimming; they must find solid footing in the pool.

Overhanging pool borders and dense marginal plants provide fish with a temporary hiding place. So do "fish houses" made from hollowed out pieces of wood or propped up stones. A pond running underneath a deck, with a solid wall above water and fish-sized openings below, is another option.

Covering the pond with netting is the surest solution for marauding birds, and has the added benefit of catching falling leaves. Netting can be added to the pond in the fall, when the vegetation that usually offers protection is depleted. An electric fence wire, fixed to insulated posts and strung completely around the pond, is very effective if carefully installed; these low-voltage units are available from hardware stores and some pool catalogs. High-pitched sound-emitting devices keep raccoons away. A motion-sensitive alarm is another option, but you'll have false alarms.

If you live in an area where there is a heron population, you'll have to take steps to protect the pond from these unwanted predators. Since herons usually wade into the water to fish, one way to deter them is to string wire about 10 to 12 inches high around the pond's edges.

Other Aquatic Life

Your garden pond can be a home for more than just fish. A wide range of aquatic life, including frogs, turtles, and even insects, either lives in water all the time, or needs a pond for part of its life cycle.

You can create an appealing environment for these creatures and either introduce them to the pond or let them find it naturally. They tend to prefer a wild environment, with plenty of plant life and insects. Depending on where you live, your pond may also attract some creatures you don't want, such as dangerous snakes or even alligators.

The following pages offer a description of the general characteristics of some aquatic life that you might want—or not want—in your pond. Beginning on page 120, you'll find a mini-encyclopedia with a selection of North American species. Of course, the species shown may not be able to survive

in your area. As well, there are local laws governing which species may be kept. Contact your local county cooperative extension office for details on species that are appropriate for your area.

If you ever decide to change the style of your water garden, do not release the creatures into a natural habitat. Adding non-native fish, amphibians, reptiles, or even plants into local habitats can upset an environment's ecological balance. For example, slider turtles, which are native to Florida, are kept as indoor pets in northern areas, and are frequently released into the wild by owners who no longer want them. These turtles cannot survive the cold, but they do live for a time, competing with native species and reducing their numbers. Contact your county cooperative extension office for help with unwanted wildlife.

Always remember that you are creating a "closed" system, an artificial environment. Many creatures will happily live there, but the balance will be somewhat different than in a truly natural aquatic environment. For example, you may introduce more, or less, of a particular species than would normally be present, without adding the appropriate number of predators for that species. Many factors affect the establishment of a balanced ecosystem. As a rule, the less you attempt to control it, the greater your chances of success.

Amphibians: In general, amphibians—frogs, toads, newts, and salamanders—are beneficial to a garden pond. They eat insects in the pond, and their spawn provide live food for fish. Some adult amphibians, in addition to eating insects, may occasionally take a small fish or two, but this is usual-

Some people find that the croaking of frogs and toads disturbs their sleep, so keep that in mind before you locate a wildlife pond close to your or your neighbor's house. The common frog (right), has no vocal sacs to amplify its croaking. It is less likely to be a nighttime nuisance.

ly a minor inconvenience, considering the benefits of the insect control they provide.

Many species of frogs and newts will live in the pond for much of their life cycle, but some, such as the wood frog, normally live on land, and use the pond only to spawn. Salamanders need an aquatic environment to spawn, but otherwise spend their life on land, buried underground. Toads also live on land and use the pond to spawn, but they're especially welcome because when they are on land, they eat insects that people don't appreciate in their gardens—earwigs, for example. A gently sloping pond edge or a slanted log will make it possible for amphibians to get in and out.

Some amphibians may find your pond on their own, or you can introduce them as eggs or tadpoles. Introducing adults often proves to be less successful. Amphibians should only be handled with wet hands, as their skin is delicate.

Reptiles: Snakes and turtles are the reptiles most commonly associated with garden ponds. As with amphibians, some live right in the water while others prefer to live near the pond.

Snakes around your pond are likely to be harmless, most proba-

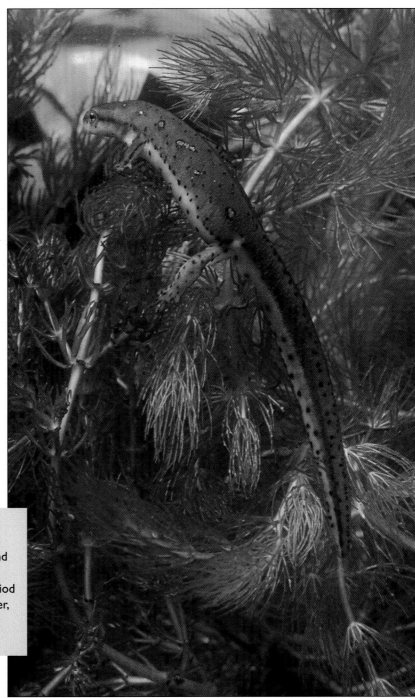

Newts, like the spotted variety at right, lay their eggs on aquatic plants, and are aquatic as adults. For a two- or three-year period of their life cycle, however, they live on land and are called efts.

bly garter snakes, which eat insects, spiders, and sometimes frogs and small fish. In some rural areas of the southeastern and southern U.S., a water moccasin or cottonmouth *(Agkistrodon piscivorus)* may find your pond. If so, get professional help to remove it. These snakes are venomous.

Adult turtles of most species that might make your pond their home are omnivorous, eating such things as plants, insects and insect larvae, algae, tadpoles, frogs, and small fish. The young are more likely to be carnivorous. Many aquatic turtles like to bask in the sun, so large flat rocks near the water's edge will be appreciated.

Insects: Whether you want them or not, your pond is likely to attract insects. Some of them, such as dragonflies and damselflies, are quite attractive in their own right. And some are fascinating to watch as they feed on other insects and even small fish.

As with other pond inhabitants, you can collect insect eggs in nearby aquatic environments—never take all of the eggs of one species as you may harm the ecosystem— or from other pond owners. But many of them are likely to appear in your pond without any effort at all on your part.

Insects and their larvae are a source of food for other pond life, including other insects. In fact, depending on what other creatures inhabit your pond, you may find it difficult to maintain an insect population in your pond.

The bright, darting color of this twelve-spot skimmer dragonfly is a welcome addition to a garden pond. Both dragonflies and damselflies lay their eggs in ponds, where the larvae stay for one or two years before emerging and transforming into the adult stage.

Attracting Birds

Chances are that some birds are already finding their way to your garden. But with a garden pond, you'll probably find that their numbers will increase. You can encourage them to stay by providing shelter and food in addition to the water your pond provides.

Water: A reliable source of clean water is always welcome to birds, both in summer and in winter. Bathing in winter helps insulate birds by keeping their feathers free of any dirt and leaving space between them for pockets of trapped air. Of course, they also need water to drink.

Most birds prefer water they can wade into, so a few rocks placed around the edges to create a shallow shelf, or a pebble beach edging at one side of the pond, will ease their access to your pond.

Shelter: By putting birdhouses in the right places, you can encourage birds who've found your garden to also stay and nest. Whether your birdhouse attracts the birds you intend it for depends to some extent on whether its dimensions,

A birdbath provides relief from summertime heat for the robin shown in the photo below. You might want a birdbath in addition to your pond, since many birds prefer shallow water; a couple of inches is adequate. A hummingbird feeder (inset) will help draw these winged marvels to your backyard. The feeder holds a mixture of water and sugar.

entrance hole, and mounting height are to the birds' liking. For example, a wren might not use a house with a 2-inch hole, because larger birds could enter and threaten the occupants. Birdhouse design is an inexact science, but some basic dimensions and mounting heights are given below. Mount the house atop a metal pole to keep cats and raccoons from reaching it. Face the entrance away from prevailing weather, and don't put the house near a feeder, because the activity makes nesting birds nervous. ➤

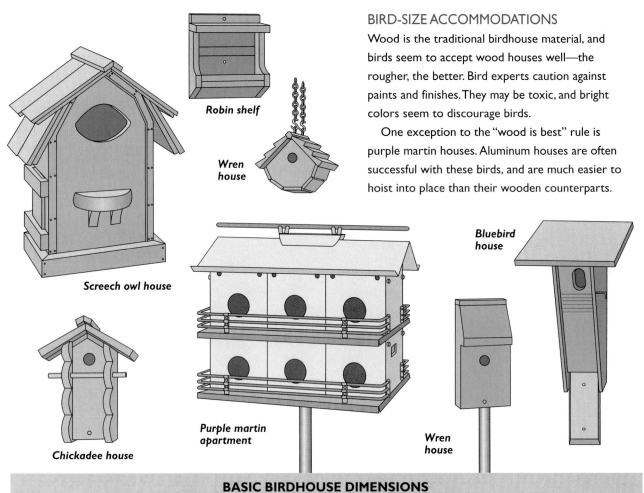

Robin shelf

Wren house

Screech owl house

Chickadee house

Purple martin apartment

Bluebird house

Wren house

BIRD-SIZE ACCOMMODATIONS

Wood is the traditional birdhouse material, and birds seem to accept wood houses well—the rougher, the better. Bird experts caution against paints and finishes. They may be toxic, and bright colors seem to discourage birds.

One exception to the "wood is best" rule is purple martin houses. Aluminum houses are often successful with these birds, and are much easier to hoist into place than their wooden counterparts.

BASIC BIRDHOUSE DIMENSIONS

	SPECIES				
	BLACK-CAPPED CHICKADEE	**BLUEBIRD**	**ROBIN**	**PURPLE MARTIN**	**SCREECH OWL**
Floor size	4"x4"	5"x5"	6"x8"	6"x6"	8"x8"
Height	8"-10"	8"	8"	6"	12"-15"
Entrance above floor	6"-8"	6"	*	1"	9"-12"
Diameter of entrance hole	1⅛"	1½"	*	2½"	3"
Height above ground	6'-15'	5'-10'	6'-15'	15'-20'	10'-30'

*One or more sides open.

Creating a Bird Habitat

In nature, birds are accustomed to the mingling of diverse plants, so variety is the key to a successful birdscape. These tips will help you create an environment similar to what occurs when a woodland and a meadow or grassland meet. This combination, with the added enticement of your pond, and perhaps even a birdbath just for them, will appeal to many of our feathered friends.

• Plant the birdscape's border with varied trees and shrubs; large shade trees for a canopy and shorter trees to form a bridge into open spaces.

• Limit lawns to small areas, placing mass plantings of graduated trees and shrubs around the lawn's perimeter. Shrubs directly bordering the lawn should branch low to the ground.

• In cold-winter regions, a stand of dense evergreen trees is ideal for winter shelter. A hedge of hemlock (*Tsuga*) can serve the same purpose.

• If you can spare a corner just for the birds, turn it into a wild area. Let grasses grow high to produce seeds, and allow a dense thorny shrub (such as *Rosa multiflora*) to grow into a tangled thicket for nesting and refuge. If a tree dies or drops a limb, leave it to decay naturally; birds will savor its insects and may use it for nesting. A naturalistic pond will fit well in a garden with a natural bird habitat like this.

This East Coast garden offers many inducements for birds in early autumn. From left to right, fading gloriosa daisies attract a pine siskin, while purple finches dip in the birdbath. Evening grosbeaks snack at a sunflower seed feeder hung from a red oak tree, and a downy woodpecker clings to a suet feeder. *Viburnum* below the tree and *Euonymus alata* in the background offer more food. The pond is close to all of these, and close enough to the blue spruce branches in the foreground, for birds to get to them for refuge, if necessary.

Food: Although your water feature will attract birds, adding a feeder increases your garden's powers of attraction. Birds often remember where they've had a good meal months before, and will return for more. Many people provide feeders in the fall, winter, and early spring. During the spring and summer, feeders are less popular, probably because birds are more territorial and chase rivals away, and because naturally available food is more appetizing. Don't expect instant success—it may be a few weeks before birds use a feeder—and keep feeders far enough from the pond that husks can't fall in it.

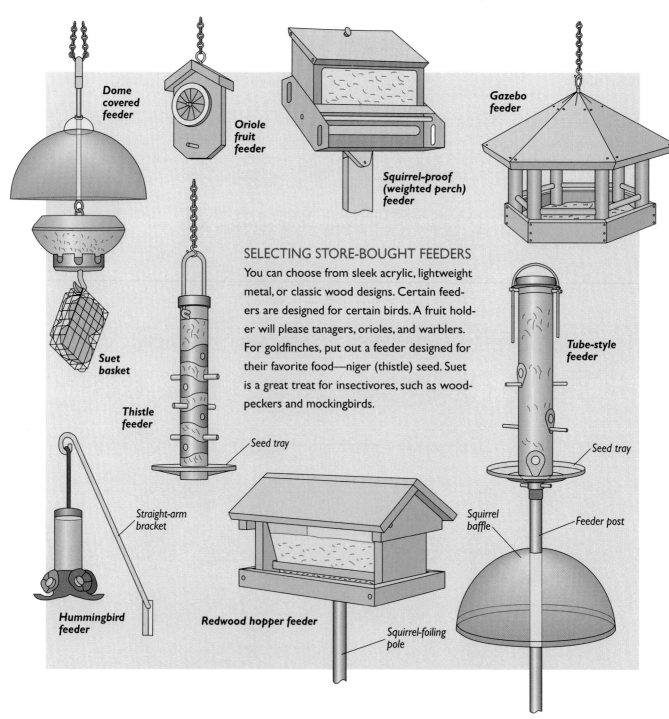

Dome covered feeder

Oriole fruit feeder

Squirrel-proof (weighted perch) feeder

Gazebo feeder

Suet basket

Thistle feeder

Tube-style feeder

SELECTING STORE-BOUGHT FEEDERS

You can choose from sleek acrylic, lightweight metal, or classic wood designs. Certain feeders are designed for certain birds. A fruit holder will please tanagers, orioles, and warblers. For goldfinches, put out a feeder designed for their favorite food—niger (thistle) seed. Suet is a great treat for insectivores, such as woodpeckers and mockingbirds.

Seed tray

Seed tray

Straight-arm bracket

Squirrel baffle

Feeder post

Hummingbird feeder

Redwood hopper feeder

Squirrel-foiling pole

A Home-built Feeder

A feeder you build yourself doesn't have to involve difficult carpentry. Most can be built with a few standard tools, such as a saw, measuring tape, and hammer. Decay-resistant woods, such as redwood or cedar heartwood, will last longest, but any scraps you have on hand will do. Keeping unwelcome visitors away from the feeder can be quite a challenge. Securing it to the top of a high pole, with a baffle below, can help.

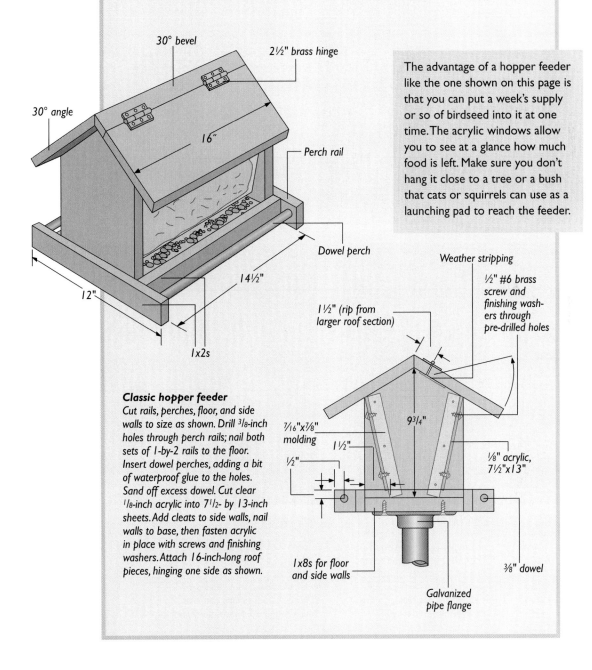

30° bevel

2½" brass hinge

30° angle

16"

Perch rail

Dowel perch

14½"

12"

1x2s

The advantage of a hopper feeder like the one shown on this page is that you can put a week's supply or so of birdseed into it at one time. The acrylic windows allow you to see at a glance how much food is left. Make sure you don't hang it close to a tree or a bush that cats or squirrels can use as a launching pad to reach the feeder.

Weather stripping

½" #6 brass screw and finishing washers through pre-drilled holes

1½" (rip from larger roof section)

7/16"x7/8" molding

1½"

9¾"

½"

⅛" acrylic, 7½"x13"

Classic hopper feeder
Cut rails, perches, floor, and side walls to size as shown. Drill 3/8-inch holes through perch rails; nail both sets of 1-by-2 rails to the floor. Insert dowel perches, adding a bit of waterproof glue to the holes. Sand off excess dowel. Cut clear 1/8-inch acrylic into 7 1/2- by 13-inch sheets. Add cleats to side walls, nail walls to base, then fasten acrylic in place with screws and finishing washers. Attach 16-inch-long roof pieces, hinging one side as shown.

1x8s for floor and side walls

⅜" dowel

Galvanized pipe flange

Encyclopedia of Pond Inhabitants

Once your garden pond is built you need to consider how you are going to stock it. Koi, goldfish, and other fish are the most common choices. But your pond may end up serving as home to a range of other creatures, including insects and spiders, reptiles, and amphibians. Some may be welcome additions; others, such as the poisonous water moccasin, need to be removed. In any case, you should know how to identify these new denizens and understand a little about them. This small encyclopedia will help you do just that.

KOI AND GOLDFISH

Kohaku
Red pattern on a white background. Indicators of exceptional koi are a bright, even red color (beni), a crisp-edged red pattern, and a snow-white background.

Taisho Sanke
A white background with red and black (sumi) pattern. The black color should be deep and lacquerlike.

Showa Sanshoku
A black background with red and white markings. It is sometimes difficult to distinguish a Showa Sanshoku from a Taisho Sanke.

Shiro Utsuri
A black and white patterned fish. The variety name is Utsurimono, which means "reflecting ones." The black pattern is considered to emerge from under the other color, which may be red, yellow, or white. The black color may extend onto the head.

Shiro Bekko
A white fish with a black pattern like stepping-stones down its back. Other background colors are red (Aka Bekko) and yellow (Ki Bekko). The black pattern usually does not extend to the head, helping to distinguish between Bekko and Utsuri.

Tancho Kohaku
A Kohaku whose only red is a spot on its head. The spot should be as neat a circle as possible, and ideally, not extend to the eyes. Other varieties may be called Tancho, such as Tancho Sanke or Tancho Showa, provided their only red is a spot on the head.

Koromo
Developed from Kohaku and Asagi varieties, these koi are similar to the Goshiki, but have a white base and Asagi-type reticulated scales on the red-patterned areas only. The name means "robed," and refers to the fact that the Asagi pattern is over the variety's normal color pattern.

Matsuba
Included in the Hikarimuji variety, these koi have a pineconelike scale pattern.

Ginrin Kohaku
This red and white Kohaku-patterned koi has the highly reflective scales of the Kinginrin variety. The full name for this variety, Kinginrin, means "golden silvery scale," although Ginrin or just Gin is a more common designation. Even metallic-scaled koi can have this type of scale.

Asagi
The back is covered in a netlike pattern of light blue or navy reticulated scales, and there is red or orange on the flanks, fins, and tail. One of the oldest varieties of koi, the Asagi has been the basis of many variations.

Doitsu (Kikusui)
Developed from a crossing with German carp, Doitsu koi may have no scales at all (called "leather carp"), or have a line of scales along their dorsal line (called "mirror carp"). Almost every variety is available in a Doitsu version.

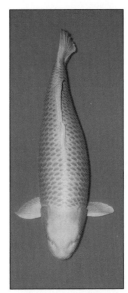

Yamabuki
A yellow koi of the Hikarimuji or Ogon variety, which are metallic-scaled koi in various colors. Platinum-colored fish are called "Purachina." The Hikarimuji variety has been crossed with many others to create metallic-scaled koi with the other color patterns.

Kujaku
A metallic koi with the reticulated scale pattern of the Asagi on its back, the Kujaku is white with a gold, yellow, orange, or red Kohaku-type pattern.

Common goldfish
The "original model" from which the fancy varieties were developed, it has short fins all round, is an excellent swimmer, and is very hardy, tolerating poorer water than many other fish.

Shubunkin
Resembles the common goldfish in shape but has matte scales with beautiful colors—a pale blue background flecked with red, blue, and black. A good choice for garden ponds.

Comet
Longer body, larger fins and more deeply forked tail fin than common goldfish. Fastest of all the fancy goldfish varieties. Does very well in outdoor pools.

OTHER FISH

Banded killifish (Fundulus diaphanus)
Description: *Back light olive, sides silver, with vertical bars.*
Size: *Up to about 3" long.*
Range: *East coast from South Carolina to Newfoundland; inland along the St. Lawrence, the Great Lakes, and the upper Mississippi.*
Habitat: *Open sandy-bottomed waters, with or without vegetation; pool margins, estuaries, tidal creeks, etc.*
Food: *Midge larvae, crustaceans, and aquatic invertebrates; grazes at all pond levels (bottom, mid, and surface).*
Life cycle: *Lives about 3 years.*
Other: *Schooling species; best to keep about 12 at a time.*

Rainbow darter (Etheostoma caeruleum)
Description: *Sides yellow and orange with 9-14 vertical bars of blue or green; head, breast, and fins green, blue, and orange.*
Size: *2"-2½" long.*
Range: *Great Lakes drainage basin; from New York State west to Minnesota; south to Alabama and Mississippi.*
Habitat: *Cool, fast-flowing streams.*
Food: *Small insects and larvae (midges, mayfly larvae), plankton.*
Life cycle: *Adults do not watch over eggs, which are laid in pebbles on the bottom, or care for young.*
Other: *Prefer moving water with abundant supply of oxygen; in home ponds, do best with waterfall, rapids, or stream.*

Mosquito fish (Gambusia affinis)
Description: *Dusky back, silvery sides, body, and fins with small black spots.*
Size: *Up to 2" long.*
Range: *East from Rio Grande to Atlantic, south from Delaware to Florida.*
Habitat: *Clear vegetated water in ponds, pools, marshes, etc.*
Food: *Insects and crustaceans.*
Life cycle: *Bears live young.*
Other: *Schooling fish.*

Bluegill sunfish (Lepomis macrochirus)
Description: *Green to olive with darker vertical bars; breast yellow in females, copper in males.*
Size: *Up to about 10" long.*
Range: *Throughout the U.S. east of the Rockies.*
Habitat: *Shallow, weedy, and warm waters of ponds and streams.*
Food: *Insects, mollusks, fish, crustaceans*
Life cycle: *Male builds nest and guards eggs during the spawning period. Introduce 1 male for 2 or 3 females. Live about 10 years.*
Other: *Can use for biological control of other fish in garden pond. One bluegill will eat all eggs of other fish.*

Three-spined stickleback (Gasterosteus aculeatus)
Description: *Silvery gray or green. Males become blue with a red belly during spawning season.*
Size: *Up to 3" long.*
Range: *From the west side of Hudson Bay east to the coast; from southern Virginia to Baffin Island; on the West Coast from the Baja peninsula to southern Alaska.*
Habitat: *Cold, clear, shallow vegetated waters.*
Food: *Small insects, crustaceans, and small fish.*
Life cycle: *Male builds a nest out of various debris, then guards eggs after the females lay them. Sticklebacks live about 4 years.*
Other: *Fairly social, but aggressively territorial. Best not to have more than 2 couples at a time.*

Golden orfe (Leuciscus idus)
Description: *Red-orange with silver sparkle. Appears slender in profile and has a terminal mouth.*
Size: *Up to 24" in a large pond.*
Range: *Not native to North America (European).*
Habitat: *Fast-swimming fish that needs a large pond. Surface dweller. Prefers deep, well-oxygenated water.*
Food: *Zooplankton and fish. Can be fed same diet as koi.*
Life cycle: *Lives about 15 years.*
Other: *Schooling species, so best if 4 or 5 are kept together. Can be trained to take food from surface.*

Spotted fishing spider (Dolomedes triton)

Description: *Greenish brown with silver white lengthwise stripes; 12 white spots on abdomen, 6 black spots between leg bases.*
Size: *Male: 3/8"-1/2"; female: 5/8"-3/4"; legspan up to 21/2".*
Range: *East of Rocky Mountains in U.S. and southern Canada.*
Habitat: *Slow-moving streams or ponds.*
Food: *Small insects, tadpoles, and small fish.*
Life cycle: *Egg sacs produced between June and September, sometimes April.*

Green darner (Anax junius)

One of the largest and fastest dragonflies. Unlike most dragonflies, green darners migrate, spending the winter in the southern U.S. (Florida), and returning north in the spring. Damselflies and dragonflies are of the order Odonata.
Description: *Freely movable heads; large compound eyes. Sharp biting mouthparts. Four wings that move independently. Dragonflies extend their wings horizontally to the sides, damselflies hold them vertically toward the rear.*
Size: *3/4"-5" long, depending on species.*
Range: *Dragonflies are found throughout North America.*
Habitat: *Various aquatic situations (ponds, marshes, slow-moving streams, etc.).*
Food: *Various flying and aquatic insects, depending on stage of life. Some naiads eat tadpoles and small fish.*
Life cycle: *Mate in flight. Eggs are deposited in or near water. Naiad spends 1 to 2 years underwater, depending on species, crawls out of water when grown and splits its skin along the midline of the thorax to release the adult.*

Giant water bug (Lethocerus americanus)

Description: *Brown color. Flattened hind legs, leathery forelegs.*
Size: *13/4"-23/8" long; 3/4"-1" broad.*
Range: *Throughout U.S. and Canada.*
Habitat: *Bottom vegetation of shallow freshwater pools and ponds.*
Food: *Insects, tadpoles, small fish, and salamanders.*
Life cycle: *Eggs are attached to plants or carried by the male on his back. Nymphs emerge in 2 weeks. Overwinter as adults.*
Other: *Will feign death if picked up. Can stab suddenly with beak.*

Diving water beetles (family Dytiscidae)

Description: *Brownish black or dark green smooth oval body. Strong, sickle-shaped jaws.*
Size: *1/16"-15/8" long. Larvae are called water tigers, measure 1/4"-23/4" long.*
Range: *Various species found throughout North America.*
Habitat: *Ponds, pools, weedy margins of rivers and streams.*
Food: *Mosquito larvae, small aquatic insects, water mites; some species will attack larger prey such as fishes, small frogs, and tadpoles.*
Life cycle: *Most lay eggs on or in aquatic plants, larvae pupate in mud near shore.*
Other: *Can stay underwater for a long time breathing air they have stored in a special chamber.*

Mayflies (order Ephemeroptera)

Description: *Brown or yellowish insects with large triangular forewings, some species have smaller rounded hind wings. Bodies are soft and have 2 or 3 tails, usually twice as long as the abdomen.*
Size: *1/8"-11/8" depending on species.*
Range: *Throughout North America; there are 550 species.*
Habitat: *Various aquatic situations.*
Food: *Naiads aquatic and omnivorous; adults terrestrial but don't eat.*
Life cycle: *The adult form has a very short life—the order name means "living a day"—some don't even live that long. Eggs are laid an hour after mating. Filaments attach them to aquatic plants or other supports. Naiads are aquatic and can live as long as 4 years.*

REPTILES

**Spotted Turtle
(Clemmys guttata)**
Description: *Black carapace with yellow spots.*
Size: *Up to 5" long.*
Range: *Eastern U.S.*
Habitat: *Bogs, brooks, pastures.*
Food: *Algae, fish, tadpoles, insect larvae, earthworms.*
Life cycle: *Lays 1 to 5 eggs in June.*

Garter snakes (genus Thamnophis)
Common name for a group of
harmless snakes.
Description: *Characterized by three
narrow, light stripes that run the length of
the darker body.*
Size: *A large garter snake may grow up
to 3' long and 1" in diameter.*
Range: *Throughout North America.*
Habitat: *Woods, rocky areas, along streams,
swamps, lakeshores.*
Food: *Insects, earthworms, slugs, tree frogs,
spiders, fish, depending on species.*
Life cycle: *Bear 6 to 25 living young
per litter.*
Other: *May dive into water when alarmed.
May secrete a foul-smelling fluid from glands
near base of tail when alarmed.*

Water snake (Nerodia sipedon)
Description: *Variable gray to reddish brown,
with large, dark brown markings on the back
and sides; belly is yellowish or reddish, spotted
with reddish-brown, rounded markings.*
Size: *Up to 53" long.*
Range: *Eastern U.S. and southeastern Canada.*
Habitat: *Near streams, marshes, rivers, lakes.*
Food: *Fish, frogs, and toads.*
Life cycle: *Bears 8 to 48 live young between June
and September.*
Other: *Can be active at temperatures lower than
those tolerated by other snakes.*

**Water moccasin or Cottonmouth
(Agkistrodon piscivorus)**
Description: *Flattened head, eyes are not visible from above.*
Size: *Up to 48" long.*
Range: *Southeastern and southern U.S.*
Habitat: *Various aquatic situations (lakes, streams, marshes, etc.).*
Food: *Snakes, turtles, amphibians, fish, mammals.*
Life cycle: *1 to 15 living young between August and October.*
Other: *Usually nocturnal. CAUTION: This snake is venomous. Contact
wildlife authorities for help in removing it.*

Blanding's turtle (Emydoides blandingi)
Description: *Dotted carapace, bright yellow patch on
lower jaw and under neck.*
Size: *Up to 9" long.*
Range: *Spotty distribution throughout eastern U.S. and Canada.*
Habitat: *Ponds, back waters, small streams, moist land.*
Food: *Omnivorous.*
Life cycle: *Lays 6 to 12 eggs between June and July,
hatchlings appear in September.*
Other: *Makes a good pet. Timid; if surprised while basking will plunge
to bottom of water and stay there for hours. Swims well.*

Green frog (Rana clamitans)
Description: *Green to brown upper may have black spots, white underparts.*
Size: *Up to 4" long.*
Range: *Southeastern Canada and eastern U.S.*
Habitat: *Swamps, brooks, streams, ponds, edges of lakes.*
Life cycle: *Females lay numerous eggs in aquatic sites.*
Vocalizations: *Low-pitched; throat swells when calling.*
Other: *Solitary. Hibernates in mud.*

Northern leopard frog (Rana pipiens)
Description: *Brown or green upper with rounded dark spots.*
Size: *Up to 4¹/₂" long.*
Range: *Southern Canada, throughout the U.S.*
Habitat: *Swamps, marshes, streams; in summer may be found in meadows.*
Life cycle: *Breeds between March and June. Lays eggs on vegetation on pond bottom.*
Vocalizations: *Variable; trills last 1-3 seconds.*

Gray tree frog (Hyla versicolor)
Description: *Gray, brown, or black with darker mottled pattern on back. Have padded suction cups on ends of toes, so they can cling to trees, branches, leaves, etc.*
Size: *Up to 2³/₈" long.*
Range: *Eastern U.S. and southeastern Canada.*
Habitat: *Marshes near woodlands, wooded stream areas. Most likely to use a garden pond for spawning if it's close to their natural habitat.*
Life cycle: *Mate in April-May. Tadpoles turn into green froglets in June.*
Other: *Turn bright green and mottled pattern disappears if warm or if sitting on something green. Patch of bright orange inside of back legs exposed when they jump.*
Vocalizations: *Call is musical trill with a bubbly quality.*

Wood frog (Rana sylvatica)
Description: *Reddish-brown or gray upper, whitish underparts. Dark mask from snout to tympanum.*
Size: *Up to 3¹/₄" long.*
Range: *Alaska, Canada, northern U.S.*
Habitat: *Damp woods.*
Life cycle: *Breeds in ponds in early spring before ice has finished melting; except for breeding it is terrestrial, hibernates in logs, under stones, etc.*
Vocalizations: *Short rasping sound almost like a clucking. Calls only during breeding season.*

Spring peeper (Hyla crucifer)
Description: *Greenish gray to reddish brown with light underparts. Dark X on its back.*
Size: *Up to 1¹/₂" long.*
Range: *Eastern U.S. and southeastern Canada.*
Habitat: *Marshes, swamps, pools; low bushes and grasses in wooded areas.*
Life cycle: *Breeds early February to March. Lays eggs in aquatic sites.*
Vocalizations: *Series of high, shrill peeps.*
Other: *Nocturnal but often calls during the day.*

American toad (Bufo americanus)
Description: *Gray to reddish brown with dark spots on cream-colored belly. Bony crests behind the eyes. 1 or 2 warts on back.*
Size: *Up to 4¹/₂" long.*
Range: *Throughout North America.*
Habitat: *Variety of situations including gardens, fields, wooded areas.*
Life cycle: *Lays eggs in strings in shallow streams or ponds.*
Other: *Nocturnal.*
Vocalizations: *High musical trill 10 to 30 seconds long.*

Building
YOUR POND

Now that you've planned your water garden—by choosing a design, selecting its materials, and deciding on the plants and fish that will make their home there—it's time to tackle the construction of your water feature. This chapter will take you through each aspect of the building process for six different types of pools—everything from assembling the tools you need to adding the water when the job is nearing completion. A separate discussion of waterfalls and streams will help demystify the process of adding these impressive features to your yard. The extensive section on edgings and borders will provide you with options for the margins of your pool. And finally, we'll walk you through the ins and outs of plumbing your pond and rigging the electrical wiring that will bring light to your new creation.

A whisk broom is handy for removing stones and smoothing the excavated surface of a garden pool. In this installation, a staked cord provides a reference for controlling the depth of the digging.

Getting Started

Building a water feature takes time and effort, but if it is done right, the result will be more than worth your labor. To ensure the best possible outcome, don't rush the job. Shortcuts will invariably end up costing you more time and money in repairs and replacement materials later. As in any project, follow this motto: Build it once—build it right. The following are a few things to consider when it comes time to build.

Legalities: Before you even lift your shovel to start digging, check local building codes and ordinances. Restrictions may include such things as pool site and surroundings, concrete construction and reinforcing, plumbing materials and installation, and electrical wiring. Also determine the locations of all public utilities, such as underground pipes and cables. If you are in any doubt about your design or your own abilities, a landscape architect, designer, or contractor should be able to provide the help you need *(page 72)*.

Talk with your neighbors about the water feature you plan to install. They may have concerns about certain aspects of the feature, such as the sound of a falls or fountain. Deal with concerns right away; they can usually be addressed easily in the planning stages but will be harder to accommodate once the pool is in place. If there will be small children in the area, you may also have to rethink your design or the need for borders or a fence.

When to build: The best time to build a water feature, particularly in cooler climates, is in the spring, at the start of the growing season. That way, you can begin planting almost as soon as you have finished building.

Plan and prepare carefully. It is best to excavate the pool on a dry, calm day. Enlist some help for this most physically demanding portion of the job or consider renting a mechanical digger or a small backhoe—it will save you a great deal of time and effort. Consult with a local rental agency for the best machine for your particular

POOL BUILDER'S CHECKLIST

FLEXIBLE LINER (see page 132)	WOOD	CONCRETE BLOCK OR BRICK
• Choose site	• Choose site	• Choose site
• Excavate for pool and marginal shelves	• Excavate floor	• Excavate footing and pool floor
• Dig trenches for drain and water supply lines	• Dig trenches for drain and water supply lines (if any)	• Dig trenches for drain and water supply lines and wiring (if any).
• Dig trenches for wiring (if any)	• Rough in plumbing and wiring (if any)	• Rough in plumbing and wiring (if any)
• Install GFCI receptacle for pump (if any)	• Select and prepare wood	• Form and pour concrete footings
• Rough in plumbing and wiring (if any)	• Assemble pool; install liner	• Build walls
• Pack excavation with 2" of sand or cover with liner protection fabric	• Fill pool; treat water as required	• Waterproof walls
• Position liner; weight edges		• Pour concrete floor or add liner
• Begin filling with water, tuck in folds		• Add veneer and/or waterproofing to walls and floor
• Trim excess liner		• Finish plumbing and wiring
• Apply edging and borders as desired		• Add edging and borders as desired
• Drain and refill pool		• Cure concrete
• Treat water as required		• Fill pool; treat water as required

excavation. If you choose this latter option, rent on a weekend when rates are lower. Be sure that there is easy access to your site.

Budgeting sensibly: Though a pool can usually be built in a weekend, don't feel obliged to complete yours on that kind of schedule. Construction can be spread over several weeks, if need be, or even over a couple of years if budget restraints prevent you from purchasing all the elements you want in one year.

One possible course is to excavate and install the pool along with a few plants in the first season. Then you can add poolside features and more elaborate plantings as desired the following year.

Remember, the pool will be a permanent feature of the backyard. Resist the temptation to modify your design dramatically to suit immediate budget concerns. It will be much more expensive to expand the pool later.

Use this same rationale when purchasing materials and buy the best. A PVC liner, for example, will be cheaper than one made from EPDM, but it may also need replacing a few years down the road.

Using a checklist: The checklists shown below will help guide you through the construction of the pool of your choice. You may wish to divide the job into several stages and make a checklist for each part, along with a list of the

tools you will need to complete it. No matter what type of pool you choose to build, consult the toolkit shown on page 130 and 131. This will help you in assembling everything you'll need for the work ahead.

Safety Tips

Always make your personal safety a primary concern whenever you are building. Here are a few tips to keep in mind:

- Wear leather gloves when handling rough materials such as stone and wood, and waterproof gloves when working with cement.
- Protect your eyes with safety goggles whenever there is a risk of flying debris, such as when hammering or sawing.
- Remove all jewelry and do not wear loose-fitting clothing when operating such machinery as a portable cement mixer or portable power tools.
- Enlist help when doing heavy lifting to avoid painful back injuries.
- Do not use power tools around a pond that is full.
- As much as possible, work during daylight hours. If you need to work at night, provide adequate lighting.

CONCRETE

- Choose site
- Excavate hole
- Dig trenches for drain and water supply lines and wiring (if any)
- Rough in plumbing and wiring (if any)
- Line excavation with gravel
- Add steel reinforcement
- Pour concrete
- Cure concrete
- Waterproof or paint concrete
- Finish plumbing and wiring
- Add edgings and borders as desired
- Fill pool; treat water as required

FIBERGLASS SHELL
(see page 134)

- Choose site
- Excavate hole
- Dig trenches for drain and water supply lines (if any)
- Dig trenches for wiring (if any)
- Install GFCI receptacle for pump (if any)
- Rough in plumbing and wiring (if any)
- Pack hole bottom with 2" of sand
- Position shell
- Backfill and add water in 4" increments
- Add edgings and border
- Drain pool; refill
- Treat water as required

The Tools for the Job

If you build your pool with a flexible liner or a fiberglass shell, you should not have to look too hard to find the tools for the job—you probably already have most of them in your home. A good shovel is a must. Even if you plan to have the pool excavated mechanically, you will almost certainly have to do some touch-up work to sculpt the surface and shelves to suit your specific needs. Likewise, marking tools are absolutely necessary. A large level, a square or T-bevel, and a tape measure or reel tape will help you to situate the pool where you want and ensure all surfaces are square and level. A wood saw will be used to make the layout stakes for any type of construction, but will also play a

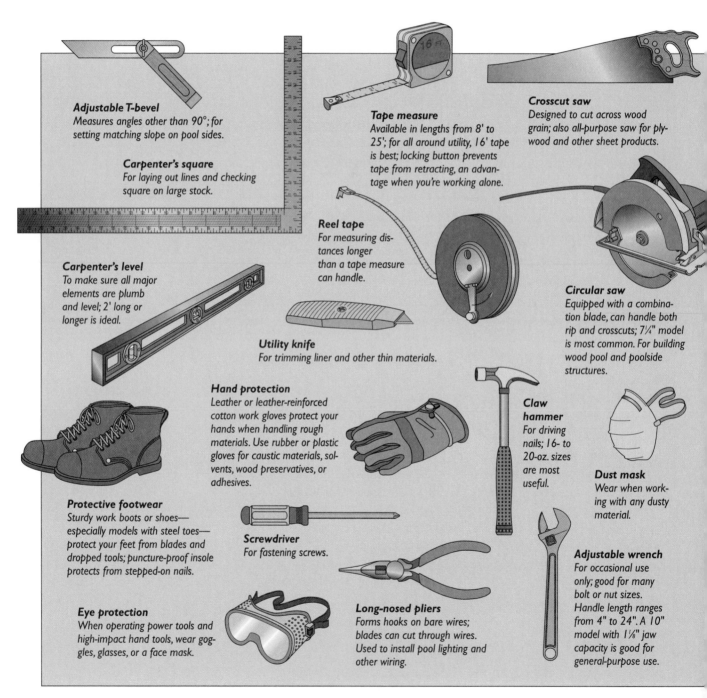

Adjustable T-bevel
Measures angles other than 90°; for setting matching slope on pool sides.

Carpenter's square
For laying out lines and checking square on large stock.

Carpenter's level
To make sure all major elements are plumb and level; 2' long or longer is ideal.

Tape measure
Available in lengths from 8' to 25'; for all around utility, 16' tape is best; locking button prevents tape from retracting, an advantage when you're working alone.

Reel tape
For measuring distances longer than a tape measure can handle.

Crosscut saw
Designed to cut across wood grain; also all-purpose saw for plywood and other sheet products.

Utility knife
For trimming liner and other thin materials.

Circular saw
Equipped with a combination blade, can handle both rip and crosscuts; 7¼" model is most common. For building wood pool and poolside structures.

Hand protection
Leather or leather-reinforced cotton work gloves protect your hands when handling rough materials. Use rubber or plastic gloves for caustic materials, solvents, wood preservatives, or adhesives.

Claw hammer
For driving nails; 16- to 20-oz. sizes are most useful.

Dust mask
Wear when working with any dusty material.

Protective footwear
Sturdy work boots or shoes—especially models with steel toes—protect your feet from blades and dropped tools; puncture-proof insole protects from stepped-on nails.

Screwdriver
For fastening screws.

Adjustable wrench
For occasional use only; good for many bolt or nut sizes. Handle length ranges from 4" to 24". A 10" model with 1⅛" jaw capacity is good for general-purpose use.

Eye protection
When operating power tools and high-impact hand tools, wear goggles, glasses, or a face mask.

Long-nosed pliers
Forms hooks on bare wires; blades can cut through wires. Used to install pool lighting and other wiring.

key role when you build any wood structure. You will also invariably need a wheelbarrow to move excavated soil out of the way, or into a formed mound which will create another feature, such as a waterfall. If you build a pool from concrete, concrete block, or brick, there is a selection of specialized tools you will need to carry out the job successfully. Some of these, like the bull float shown among the collection of tools below, will have to be built on the job.

Always make sure your tools are in good working order—blades should be sharp and handles secure. During the planning stage, make a list of the tools you will need for each stage of construction and assemble them before you begin.

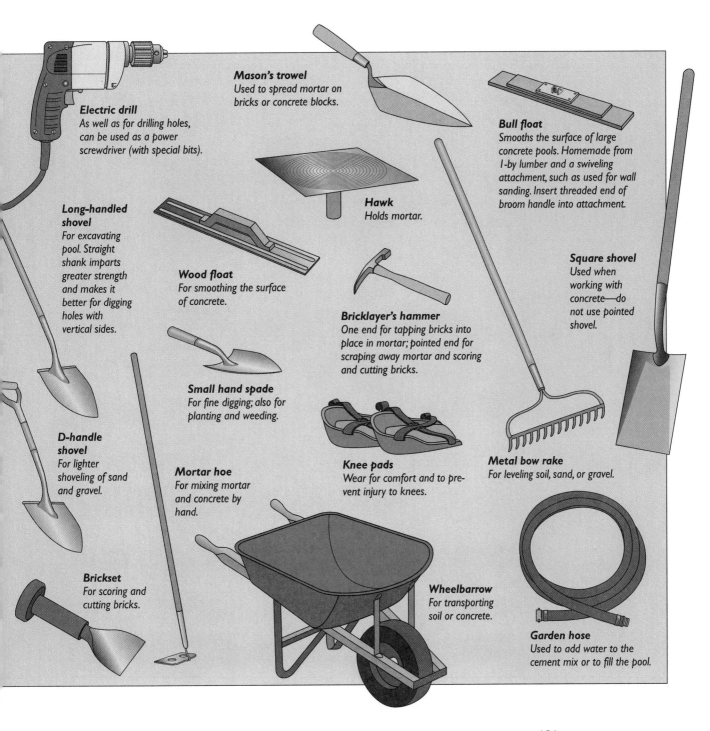

Electric drill
As well as for drilling holes, can be used as a power screwdriver (with special bits).

Mason's trowel
Used to spread mortar on bricks or concrete blocks.

Bull float
Smooths the surface of large concrete pools. Homemade from 1-by lumber and a swiveling attachment, such as used for wall sanding. Insert threaded end of broom handle into attachment.

Long-handled shovel
For excavating pool. Straight shank imparts greater strength and makes it better for digging holes with vertical sides.

Hawk
Holds mortar.

Wood float
For smoothing the surface of concrete.

Square shovel
Used when working with concrete—do not use pointed shovel.

Bricklayer's hammer
One end for tapping bricks into place in mortar; pointed end for scraping away mortar and scoring and cutting bricks.

Small hand spade
For fine digging; also for planting and weeding.

D-handle shovel
For lighter shoveling of sand and gravel.

Mortar hoe
For mixing mortar and concrete by hand.

Knee pads
Wear for comfort and to prevent injury to knees.

Metal bow rake
For leveling soil, sand, or gravel.

Brickset
For scoring and cutting bricks.

Wheelbarrow
For transporting soil or concrete.

Garden hose
Used to add water to the cement mix or to fill the pool.

Flexible Liner Pools

Because of their flexibility, relatively low cost, and ease of installation, flexible liners are the most popular material used in water garden construction today. With the proper planning and preparation, there is no reason you shouldn't be able to install a moderately sized liner pool in the course of a weekend with a fairly small outlay.

The vast majority of liners are made from either polyolefin, polyvinyl chloride (PVC), or synthetic rubber (EPDM). The latter material is the most expensive, but it is also the most durable. If you can afford it, it is by far the best choice.

When it comes to buying a liner, you have two options. You can purchase a precut rectangle of the size you need and then trim it to make a precise fit, or you can order a liner sized to fit your pool.

To determine the size of liner you'll need for a naturally shaped pond like the one shown below, draw an imaginary rectangle around it and measure length and width. To each of these measurements, add twice the pond's maximum depth plus 2 feet to give you the necessary surplus of material to extend beyond the edge of the excavated area.

If you are excavating an area of lawn, keep the uprooted sod in a shady place until the pool is finished. You will be able to use it later for patching bare spots around the border. Remember, rough plumbing and wiring installations should be completed before sand is added to the excavated surface. These concerns are addressed beginning on page 158.

Installing a flexible liner

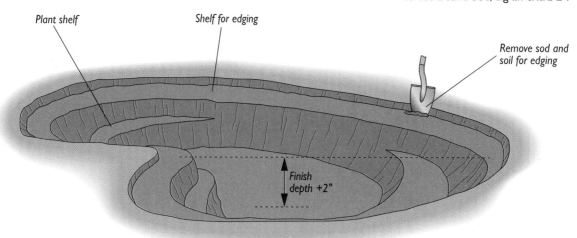

Stake hose in place

Plant shelf

Shelf for edging

Remove sod and soil for edging

Finish depth +2"

1 Marking and excavating
With a garden hose or a length of rope, trace the intended outline of your pool, allowing 2" extra all around for a layer of sand or a buffer of liner protection fabric. Survey the outline to be sure it is what you want, then install stakes around it to mark the curves *(left)*. Then dig around the outline, creating a shallow shelf for the edging *(below)*. Next, dig out shelves for plants; 10" to 12" wide is common. Continue digging out the main area, measuring the depth as you go with a tape measure or a marked stake. If you're planning to use a sand bed, dig an extra 2".

2 Leveling the rim

As you excavate, use a length of 2x4 and a level to check to ensure that the rim of the pool is perfectly level from edge to edge *(right)*. Any discrepancy might leave the liner exposed and vulnerable to abrasion and deterioration. For a larger pool that cannot be spanned easily by a 2x4, drive a center stake and use it as a pivot to measure out to all sides. To adjust the rim, simply rework the high side or build up the low side slightly.

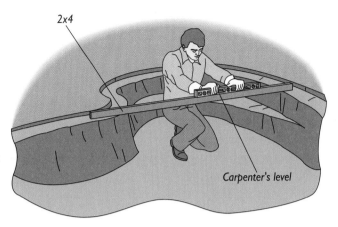

2x4

Carpenter's level

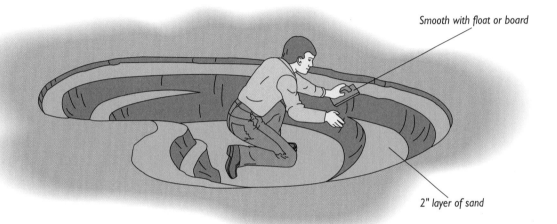

Smooth with float or board

2" layer of sand

3 Smoothing the surface

To protect the liner, remove all rough edges—roots, rocks, and debris—from the excavated area, fill any holes, and tamp down soft soil. Lay a 2" layer of sand (or install a sheet of liner protection fabric) over all surfaces. Spread the sand evenly, packing it into place, and smooth the surface with a board or a concrete float *(above)*.

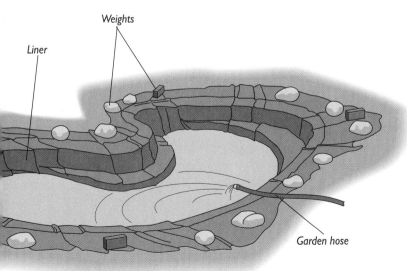

Weights

Liner

Garden hose

4 Positioning the liner and filling the pool

Warm up the liner by stretching it out in the sun. This will soften the material. If you need to make a seam, do so now using the solvent cement and method recommended by the liner manufacturer. Next, with helpers, spread the liner loosely over the hole. Flapping it up and down will force air under the liner and help float it into place. Make sure the liner overlaps the edges evenly; tight curves may require folded pleats. Weight down the edges with heavy stones or bricks and slowly begin filling the pond with a garden hose *(left)*. Once the pond is nearly full, begin setting the edging into place *(page 144)*.

Preformed Shells

When it comes to ease of installation, nothing can top a preformed shell. The only question is whether you'll find the shape you want or the right dimensions for any fish or plants you plan to include in your water garden, but that rarely poses a problem today. Shells are available in a wide array of shapes, depths, and sizes. They can even be used for semiraised or sloping sites, though you may need to build a retaining wall in advance for these installations *(page 154)*.

The keys to successful installation are maintaining level surfaces and providing solid support for the relatively weak fiberglass. As with any pool excavation, if you are working on grass, remove the sod and keep it in a shady place to use for patching holes later. Remember that rough plumbing and wiring installations should be completed before sand is added to the excavated surface. The basics of these tasks are addressed on page 158.

Building a pool with a preformed shell

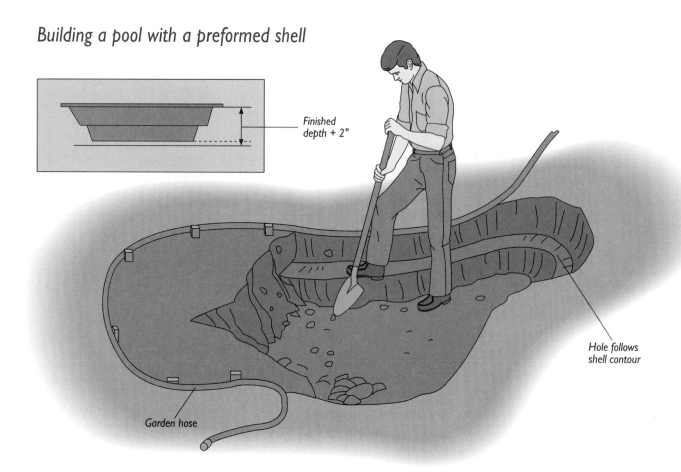

Finished depth + 2"

Hole follows shell contour

Garden hose

1 Marking and digging the hole
Flip the shell upside down and outline its top edge in the desired location on the ground using a hose or length of rope. Add 2" all around to accommodate the layer of sand you will add later. Drive stakes around the outline to keep the hose in place, remove the shell, and start digging. Make sure the excavation follows the same general taper as the shell walls, which will take some careful measuring and digging. If your shell includes a marginal shelf, shape this too, again leaving 2" all around. Take particular care with the depth and shape of the hole's bottom.

134

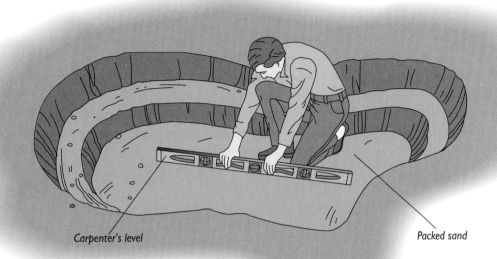

Carpenter's level

Packed sand

2 Checking for level

Once the hole is roughed out, check the bottom with a carpenter's level and make any necessary adjustments. Also remove any sharp objects such as rocks or roots, filling any gaps left behind. Next, add a 2" layer of clean, damp sand. Spread it carefully along the bottom and check again for level *(above)*.

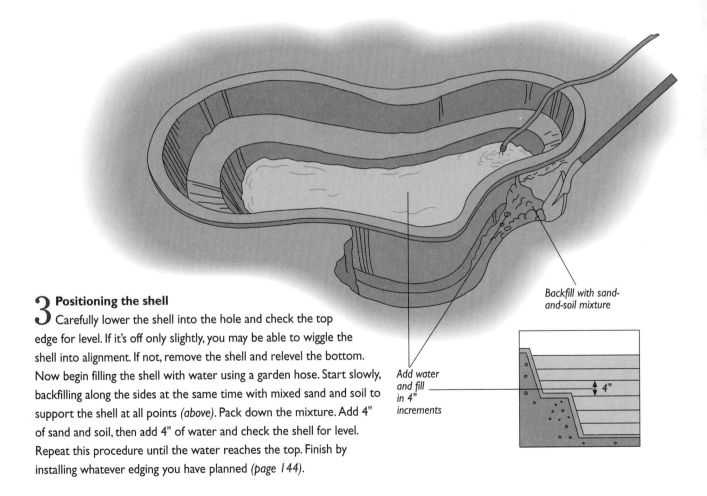

Backfill with sand-and-soil mixture

Add water and fill in 4" increments

4"

3 Positioning the shell

Carefully lower the shell into the hole and check the top edge for level. If it's off only slightly, you may be able to wiggle the shell into alignment. If not, remove the shell and relevel the bottom. Now begin filling the shell with water using a garden hose. Start slowly, backfilling along the sides at the same time with mixed sand and soil to support the shell at all points *(above)*. Pack down the mixture. Add 4" of sand and soil, then add 4" of water and check the shell for level. Repeat this procedure until the water reaches the top. Finish by installing whatever edging you have planned *(page 144)*.

Concrete Pools

If you have never worked with concrete before, it shouldn't be your first choice of water garden materials. Concrete is more difficult to work with than flexible liners and fiberglass shells. It is also prone to cracking in colder climates. Still, done properly, concrete can create durable free-form natural pools *(below)* and formal raised ones *(page 138)*.

For anything larger than a tiny accent pool, you should probably use premixed concrete, either carted home on a rental trailer or delivered to the site. Ask for 4- or 5-sack concrete with pea gravel, and request it a little on the dry side. The concrete supplier should be able to help you pick the exact mix. For a large pour, you may need a pump to reach the site from the street. For information on curing concrete, see opposite page.

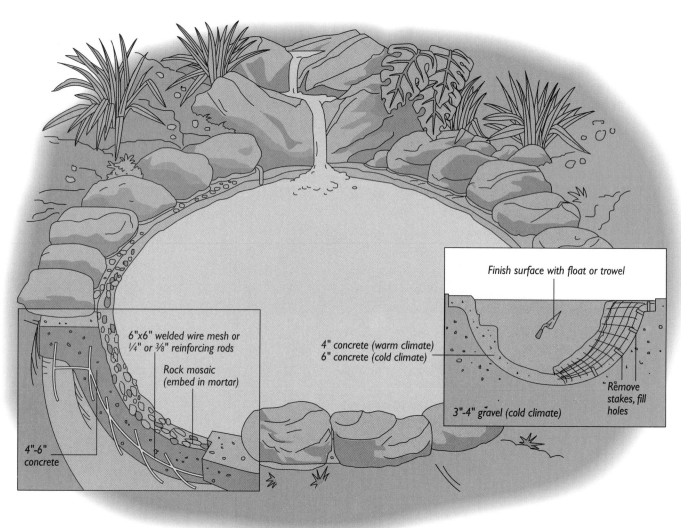

6"x6" welded wire mesh or ¼" or ⅜" reinforcing rods

Rock mosaic (embed in mortar)

4"-6" concrete

4" concrete (warm climate)
6" concrete (cold climate)

Finish surface with float or trowel

Remove stakes, fill holes

3"-4" gravel (cold climate)

BUILDING A FREE-FORM CONCRETE POOL

Begin by excavating and compacting the pool site. In areas of extreme cold, allow an additional 3" to 4" for a layer of gravel under the concrete. Walls must be sloped—45 degrees is about the limit. To prevent runoff from entering the pool, allow for a 1" or 2" perimeter lip. Add reinforcing in the form of wire mesh or rods. Then drive stakes in every square foot to indicate the depth of the concrete. Pour the concrete and finish the job as shown in the inset illustration above.

Moist-curing is the process of keeping a concrete surface wet while the material slowly hardens, producing a stronger structure. It's also a good way to rid the new pool of its supply of free lime, which is toxic to plant and fish life. One method is to fill the new pool with water and let it sit for 24 hours. Drain and refill, repeating the process three or four times. The last time, let the water stand for a week and then rinse the pool thoroughly.

As a quick alternative, simply apply two coats of a commercial, cement-based waterproofing compound. To impart color to the cement, use a water-base epoxy paint.

Prepare the surface in this way: While the concrete is damp but fully set, etch it with muriatic acid, mixing one part acid with two parts tap water in a nonmetallic bucket. Using a long-handled brush, slosh the acid onto all surfaces. Scrub until the acid ceases to bubble and the concrete attains a uniform, open-grained texture similar to that of fine sandpaper. Wash the acid off and flush it out of the pool.

Paint should be applied with a brush or roller to a clean surface. Then paint according to the manufacturer's instructions. Let the paint dry for 14 days before filling the pool.

Working with Shotcrete

Shotcrete is a mixture of hydrated cement and aggregate that is applied over and under a reinforcing grid directly against the soil. The mix is shot from a nozzle under pressure, allowing complete freedom of size and shape, since it follows any excavated contour. Shotcrete comes in both "wet-mix" and "dry-mix" versions.

Because of the specialized equipment involved, this is a contractor-only job. Still, an industrious homeowner can do the excavation and prep work, then call in the contractor for the final application to reduce the cost of the operation. To minimize the effects of overspray, cover the surrounding area with plastic sheeting or other dropcloths.

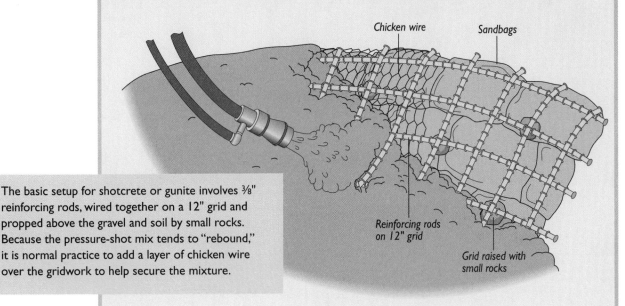

Chicken wire

Sandbags

Reinforcing rods on 12" grid

Grid raised with small rocks

The basic setup for shotcrete or gunite involves ⅜" reinforcing rods, wired together on a 12" grid and propped above the gravel and soil by small rocks. Because the pressure-shot mix tends to "rebound," it is normal practice to add a layer of chicken wire over the gridwork to help secure the mixture.

Concrete Formwork

Although largely replaced by gunite where fluid shapes are required, and by concrete blocks where they're not, formed concrete is still preferred by many for its crisp edges. Even a brick or block pool requires a poured footing as a base.

The easiest way to construct a footing is simply to dig a trench and pour concrete in place. In cases where the earth is too soft or too damp to hold a vertical edge, you can build a simple form. The footing must be flat on top if a block wall is to be built on it *(page 139)*. If you're constructing a sunken pool, you may be able to dispense with wall forms if the soil is firm enough to stand without crumbling.

Note that the illustrations below are based on the requirements of a nonfrost region, where the top of the footing can be nearly flush with the ground. Be sure to check local codes for the footing requirements where you live.

Before pouring the concrete, you may need to add reinforcing rods to both footing and wall forms. Once the footings and walls have set, lay down 6-by-6-inch welded wire mesh in the floor area and pour a 4-inch concrete slab.

If you are building a raised or semiraised pool, you can cast the walls at the same time as the footings. To use the combination form seen at left, dig a trench for the footings and erect the wall form around the pool perimeter as shown. Lay a gravel base and pour the form using the guidelines provided with the illustrations at left and below.

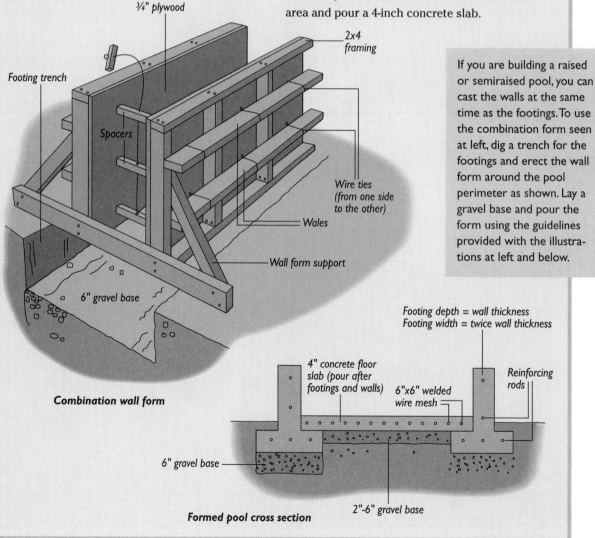

¾" plywood

2x4 framing

Footing trench

Spacers

Wire ties (from one side to the other)

Wales

Wall form support

6" gravel base

Combination wall form

Footing depth = wall thickness
Footing width = twice wall thickness

4" concrete floor slab (pour after footings and walls)

6"x6" welded wire mesh

Reinforcing rods

6" gravel base

2"-6" gravel base

Formed pool cross section

Concrete Block Pools

For fast, inexpensive masonry wall construction, it's hard to beat concrete blocks. These rugged units make strong cores for formal pools or fountains; for a warmer appearance, you can easily veneer them with brick, stone, or tile *(below)*.

Once you have the boundaries of your pool staked out, but before you begin building, lay a dry course of blocks to make sure you don't end up doing any unnecessary cutting. To tie in the corners, it is best to overlap full blocks at each corner *(see step 3, top)*. Also note that the cross webs of concrete blocks are thicker on one side; always lay blocks with the thick webs facing up. This provides more surface for the bed of mortar.

Keep your mortar a bit on the thick side; a good recipe is ½ part portland cement, 1 part masonry cement and 4½ parts masonry sand. Don't wet the blocks, as you would with a brick structure. The stiffer mortar and the lower rate of absorption of the blocks will keep them from soaking up too much water from the mortar.

Building a concrete block pool

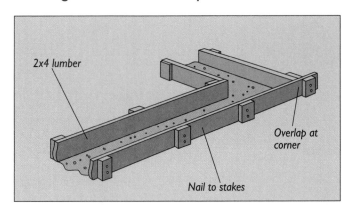

2x4 lumber

Overlap at corner

Nail to stakes

1 Making the footing
With wood stakes and cord, lay out the perimeter of the pool. Use the cords as guides to excavate a trench for the footing. Check that it is of even width and depth all around. If you dig too deep, do not backfill; allow the concrete to fill the area. If the earth is firm and dry, you can pour the concrete into the trench. If the earth is too soft to hold a vertical edge, build a wood form like the one shown at left. Make it from 2x4 lumber, overlapping at the corners and ensuring it is perfectly level.

Adding Strength and Beauty

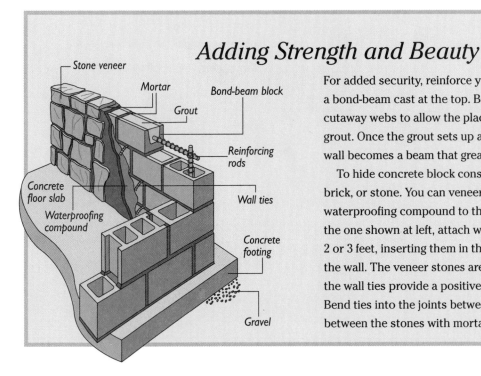

Stone veneer

Mortar

Grout

Bond-beam block

Reinforcing rods

Concrete floor slab

Waterproofing compound

Wall ties

Concrete footing

Gravel

For added security, reinforce your concrete block walls with a bond-beam cast at the top. Bond-beam blocks come with cutaway webs to allow the placement of reinforcing rods and grout. Once the grout sets up around the steel, the top of the wall becomes a beam that greatly strengthens the wall.

To hide concrete block construction, veneer it with tile, brick, or stone. You can veneer over a liner or just apply a waterproofing compound to the wall. For a stone veneer like the one shown at left, attach wall ties to the block wall every 2 or 3 feet, inserting them in the mortar joints as you build the wall. The veneer stones are then installed with mortar; the wall ties provide a positive connection to the mortar. Bend ties into the joints between stones, then fill the spaces between the stones with mortar.

2 Starting the first partial course

Pour the footing and allow the concrete to cure for at least two days. Snap a chalk line to mark the outer edge of the wall. Then, starting at one corner, lay a 2" thick mortar bed long enough for four blocks. Lay the corner block carefully and press it down to an accurate ⅜" joint with the foundation. Spread mortar on the ends of the next blocks and place them, allowing a ⅜" mortar joint between them *(right)*. Repeat the process, starting at the same corner and laying three blocks in the other direction.

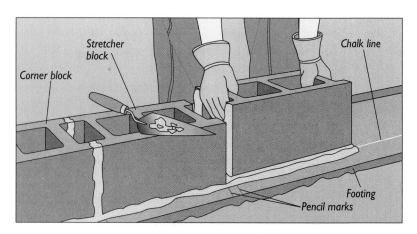

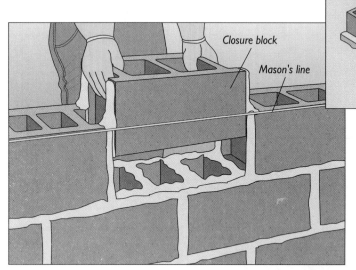

3 Filling in the wall

Make leads—partial courses—at all four corners of the wall, making sure to tie them in *(above)*. Then, fill in the walls between the leads, keeping a careful check on the ⅜" joint spacing. Check alignment, level, and plumb frequently as you go. To fit the closure block, spread mortar on all edges of the opening and the ends of the block, then carefully set it in place *(left)*.

4 Capping the wall

When the walls are finished, spread the liner over the pool and begin slowly filling the pool with a garden hose *(inset)*. Monitor the process carefully to ensure the liner is evenly placed and does not snag on the pool walls. Trim the liner and fold it over the top of the wall so that it will be trapped under the cap blocks. Spread mortar on top of the wall and tap the cap blocks in place *(above, right)*, checking carefully for level as you go. Continue along the entire pool until the cap is in place and the liner is secured. Then, finish the joints with a sled jointer, tooling the vertical joints first, then the horizontal joints. Finally, slide your trowel along the wall to remove mortar that has squeezed out of the joints.

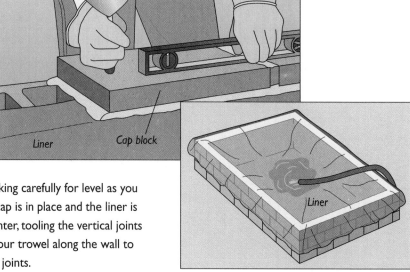

Raised Pools Made from Bricks

If you have never worked with brick, constructing a brick pool is probably not a good first project—high-quality work is crucial here to ensure that the structure is soundly built. If you have some experience with this type of masonry, however, the following steps will help you build a solid, attractive raised pool. The steps shown are for a common bond brick pattern, but the information on brick patterns below should enable you to construct the other styles. Check local codes first to determine whether your pool will need reinforcement. And wear work gloves when working with brick to protect your hands.

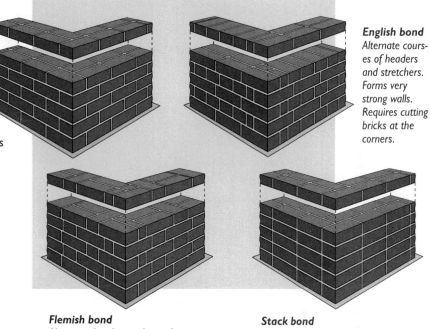

Running bond
Easy to lay. Mainly used for veneers and single-thickness partitions. Double thicknesses must be linked with metal ties.

English bond
Alternate courses of headers and stretchers. Forms very strong walls. Requires cutting bricks at the corners.

Flemish bond
Alternates headers and stretchers in each course. Both decorative and structural.

Stack bond
Usually used for decorative effect in veneers. Weak; must be liberally reinforced if it is to be used structurally.

BRICK BOND PATTERNS

Four of the most common brick patterns are shown at right. Each one requires a particular corner treatment. For English and Flemish bond, as well as common bond shown in the step below, you will have to cut bricks to finish each course, called closure bricks. Check with local building authorities before making a final decision on a bond pattern; if your wall requires steel reinforcing, some bonds may be more adaptable than others.

Building a brick pool

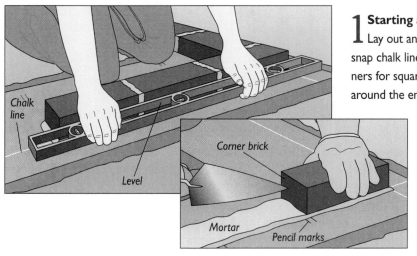

Chalk line

Level

Corner brick

Mortar

Pencil marks

1 Starting a corner lead
Lay out and pour concrete footings *(page 139)*. Then snap chalk lines to mark the pool walls and check the corners for square. Lay a single course of bricks in a dry run around the entire pool. Adjust the joint width between bricks so you have as little cutting to do as possible. Mark the joint spaces on the footing. Spread mortar for the first three bricks and place the first one precisely at the corner *(inset)*. Lay the remaining four lead bricks, checking carefully for accuracy. Use a level to check level and plumb, as well as the bricks' alignment *(left)*.

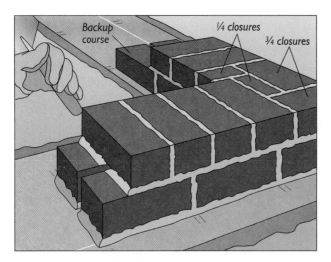

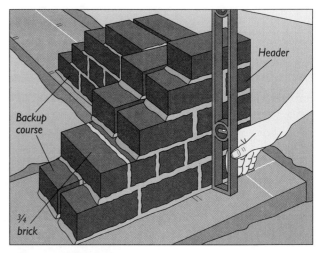

2 Starting the header course

Spread mortar and lay the backup course inside the front course. Make sure not to disturb the front course, and remember that there is no mortar joint between these courses. Check that the backup course is level with the first one. Then take two bricks and cut them into ¾ and ¼ closures. Lay them as shown and complete the lead header course *(above)*.

3 Completing the lead

Now lay the leads for the next three stretcher courses. Note that each of these courses is the same as the first course, except the fourth course, which begins with a header. Check your completed lead for accuracy, and repeat Steps 2 and 3 at the other corners of the pool. Then proceed to Step 4 to begin filling in the walls between the leads.

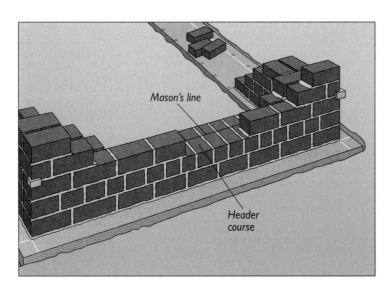

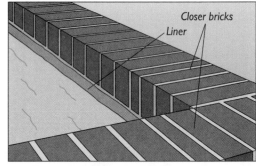

4 Filling in

Stretch a mason's line between two completed leads as shown. Then begin laying the interior wall bricks, first filling the front, or outer, course, then the backup, or inner, course. Keep the line about ¹⁄₁₆" away from the bricks and flush with their top edges. Lay bricks from both ends toward the middle *(above)*. Continue to the top of the wall, then fill between the remaining pairs of leads.

5 Adding the cap

Lay the liner in the pool as for a concrete block pool *(page 140)*. Then install a rowlock cap—a row of header bricks placed on edge. Lay them out dry first, allowing for the mortar joints—notice how the corner is treated in the illustration above. Trim the final bricks flush with the edges of the wall or cut closer bricks, if necessary. Trim the liner and fold it about halfway cross the top row of bricks, then spread mortar and lay the cap bricks *(above)*. Use plants or a veneer *(page 139)* to conceal the liner above the water.

Wooden Raised Pools

If constructing a masonry pool seems like a daunting task, consider working with wood. Built from 4-by-4 timbers stacked and secured together with threaded rods, the model shown below can be assembled in a few hours. Rot-resistant woods like western red cedar are preferable for this kind of pool, since they stand up well to the elements. Railroad ties are also a popular choice, but some people dislike the smell of the creosote that is used to preserve them. Pressure-treated lumber can also be used, but like railroad ties, it contains potentially harmful chemicals and should not contact the water.

Building a pool with wood

1 Assembling the frame
Cut the beams to length for the sides of the pool, then dry-assemble them to test the fit. It is crucial that the side beams overlap as shown. This will ensure that the threaded rods will help hold the assembly together properly. Mark and drill holes through the center of the beams for threaded rods, locating one rod at each corner and one at the midpoint of each side as shown. Countersink the holes on the top and bottom of the pool sides to accommodate the nuts and washers that will secure the rods. Choose the location for the pool, excavate the floor area, and assemble the frame in place, screwing the nuts on one end of the rods and tightening with a wrench.

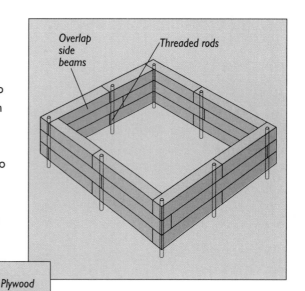

Overlap side beams

Threaded rods

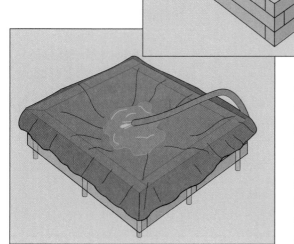

Plywood lining

2" layer of sand

2 Preparing for a liner
Cut plywood or foam to line the sides of the pond and set it in place. There's no need to secure the material to the pool side—the water pressure will hold it in place. Then, spread a 2" layer of sand across the bottom of the pool to protect the liner.

3 Fastening the liner
Spread the liner over the pool and begin slowly filling the pool with water. Monitor the process carefully to ensure that the liner is evenly placed and does not snag on the pool walls. When the pool is full, trim the liner and fold it in several pleats so it extends about halfway across the top beams. Cut capping boards from the same stock or from slightly thinner boards (if you used 4x4 beams, you can use 2x4 capping). Fasten the capping boards atop the pool sides, nailing through the folded liner.

Edgings and Borders

Edgings and borders perform a practical and an esthetic role in the water garden, both hiding and protecting the liner or shell and enhancing the overall effect of the pool. Ideally, a border should link the water garden with its surroundings. Carefully observe the pathways and natural stones around the pond when selecting the edging you will use. The following section will highlight more than a dozen edging options, providing a choice of both method and materials.

BOULDERS AND STONE

Framing a garden with large boulders is not an easy job, but the results can be rewarding. Look for native stones that mirror the natural landscape. Because moving these large rocks can be difficult work, it's best to keep a few back-saving tips in mind: If possible, break the stones with a sledge-hammer and move them piece by piece, reassembling them in place with cement slurry; slide them on a large shovel, chain-link fencing,

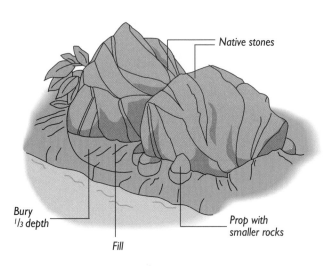

Native stones

Bury
1/3 depth

Fill

Prop with
smaller rocks

BOULDER EDGINGS

Boulders appear most natural when partially buried. Otherwise, prop them up on smaller stones, and pack the area with soil and plantings *(left)*. As another option, submerge the boulders partially in water by placing them on a marginal shelf inside the pool *(below)*.

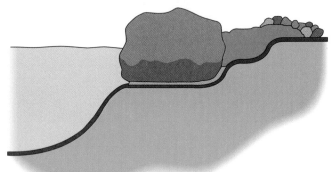

Installing a fieldstone edging

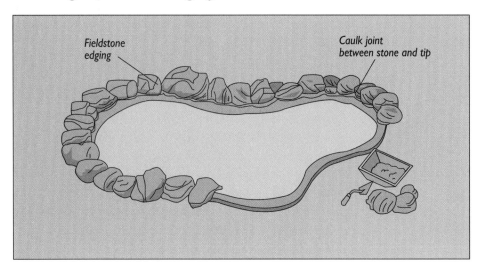

Fieldstone
edging

Caulk joint
between stone and tip

Lay fieldstones out in a dry run, arranging them in a pleasing pattern. Then, mix some mortar (three parts sand and one part cement) and fix them in place one stone at a time using a trowel *(left)*.

or board; or roll them using a steel bar or wood plank as a lever. Fieldstones impart an equally natural look. They can be secured with a small amount of mortar as shown on the facing page.

FLAGSTONE AND TILE

In natural ponds, masonry is the number one choice for making the transition between water and land. Laying flagstone is similar to installing a fieldstone edging. The first step is arranging the stones in a pleasing pattern, cutting them as necessary with a brickset. The steps for laying flagstone edging are shown on page 146. Bricks and pavers, two other options, are laid in the same manner. A selection of masonry edgings is shown below.

Ceramic tile is another popular edging option, though it finds most use in formal pools. Poured concrete, concrete block, and brick all make acceptable surfaces for tile. The tile itself should be a vitreous (nonabsorbent) type for any area that comes into contact with the water. When installing tile, or any other type of paving stones, consider the surface texture. Smooth, shiny surfaces often prove to be slippery when wet. Remember, in flexible liner ponds, you need to protect the liner from damage. This can be accomplished by allowing the edging to hang a few inches over the edge (which may necessitate using large pavers) or by planting large-leaved marginals around the pond. ➤

Brick
A traditional surface. Needs to be reworked after severe freezes.

MASONRY EDGINGS

Formal pools can be edged with a variety of masonry options. All of the styles shown here are wet mortared in the same manner as the flagstone edging shown on page 146.

Mexican pavers
Octagonal units have a grainy, hand-crafted look. Small squares complete the pattern.

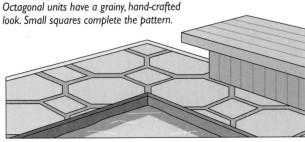

Tile
Creates a more formal effect and a smoother, more reflective surface.

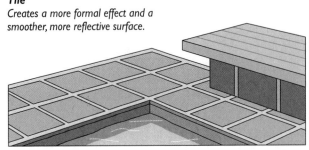

Adobe
Its rounded, massive form makes an attractive feature alongside a pool.

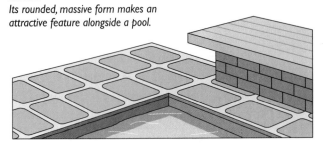

Stone
Rugged finish resists scratches and stains; gives a rough-hewn effect.

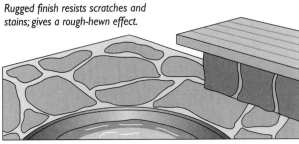

Laying flagstone edging

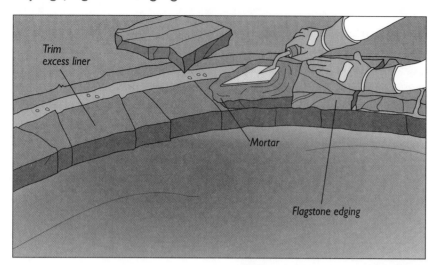

Trim
excess liner

Mortar

Flagstone edging

1 Laying the edging
With the pool filled, trim the liner so it extends about 4" to 5" over the edging shelf. Lay a dry run of stones and do any necessary cutting so the edging fits perfectly. Then, spread a thin layer of mortar on the shelf and set the stones in place one at a time.

2 Bedding the stones
With the stones firmly in place, bed each one by tapping it with a rubber mallet. Use a straightedge and level to maintain an even surface.

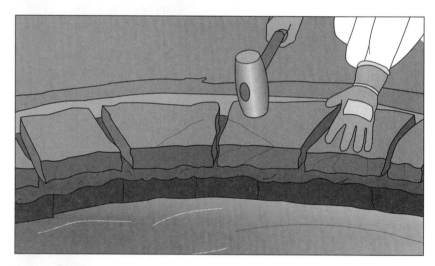

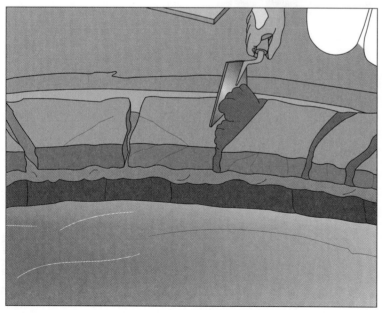

3 Filling the joints
Let the mortar set for 24 hours, then pack mortar between the stones. Add one-half part fireclay to the mortar to improve workability. Smooth the joints with a pointing trowel and clean up spills with a sponge and water. Muriatic acid washes, commonly used to clean cured masonry, can be used except with limestone and marble; the acid mars these types of stone.

WOOD EDGING

Wood is another popular pond edging material. Some options are shown below. As in wood pools, use a naturally rot-resistant species if possible. Hardwoods such as oak are best. Softwoods such as western red cedar are usable, although they may need to be coated with a protective sealant. To minimize water damage, position wood edgings so that rainwater runs off rather than forming pools. For a more natural appearance, leave bark on wood posts and logs. Modern pool builders are afforded yet another option: imitation concrete logs. Within a fairly short time they will become covered by moss and appear remarkably natural. Pressure-treated woods and railroad ties also can be used, but they contain potentially harmful chemicals and should not contact the water. ➤

MINIATURE PILINGS

Wood posts or logs, in diameter ranging from 2" to 6", can be used to form a series of miniature pilings. Set the lengths vertically and butted tightly against one another. Epoxy can be used to fill the spaces between the logs. The bottom ends should be secured in concrete footings with additional concrete support behind.

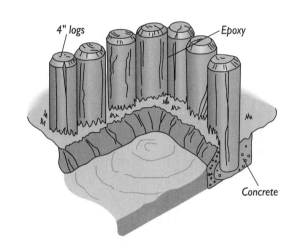

Two types of wood edgings

Upright wood edging

Cement is not necessary for securing upright wood edging, but for the installment shown at right, you will need to plan ahead. When the pool is being excavated, dig a trench around the border to fit the logs snugly. Lay sand or a liner protection fabric in the trench and set the logs upright. Backfill behind the log to finish.

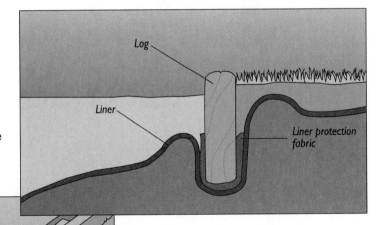

Two-by-four and benderboard edging

Two-by-fours can be staked in place to line a shallow, gravel-edged pool, and serve as a transition between the pool and the surrounding lawn. Benderboard is used where the border curves. Be sure to wet the benderboard before shaping, and secure it to stakes every 6" to 8".

PEBBLE BEACHES

Pebble beaches are suitable for ponds with gradually sloping sides or those that have a wide, shallow shelf or bog area around the perimeter.

River pebbles or gravel are the most common materials used. Remember to wash them thoroughly before adding them to the pool. If the gravel is sharp, you may need to lay down a sheet of liner protection fabric in between it and the liner. Your method of installing a pebble beach will differ depending on whether you want the pebbles to line the entire bottom of the pond or whether you'd rather confine them to the edge. Both methods are illustrated below. In some cases, you may decide to add a thin layer of cement over the pebbles to prevent them from slipping into the pond, or from being lifted and tossed into the pool.

TURF EDGING

Turf is a common edging for natural ponds but there are several concerns specific to this design.

Pebble beaches

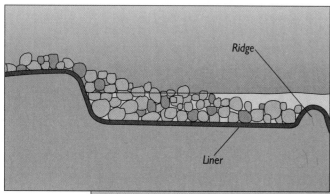

Pebble shelf
Pebbles are located on a wide shelf at the perimeter of the pond. A ridge of earth prevents them from slipping into the water.

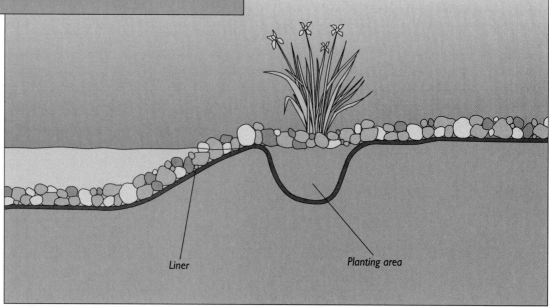

Pebble beach
Pebbles cover a gently sloping pond edge. A trench filled with earth serves as a planting area for bog or moisture-loving plants.

First, the grass will have to be cut by hand to prevent the grass cuttings from getting into the water. In addition, the edge of a liner pond may need some extra support so that it does not slowly erode and collapse into the pond. Two methods of providing this added support are illustrated below. Even if support is not an issue, you will still have to consider providing adequate drainage in order to prevent the lawn from flooding in the event of a heavy rain. The drainage technique illustrated at the bottom of this page should solve any such water accumulation problems.

Allowing for turf edging

Two ways to support a liner in a grass-edged pool
To support steep sides, lay large, flat stones on edge. The stones should be secured in place with a thin bed of mortar. Trim the liner flush with the top of the stone *(right)*. For turf-edged pools with a gently sloping shelf, lay a thin bed of mortar and set medium-size stones up to the edge *(below)*.

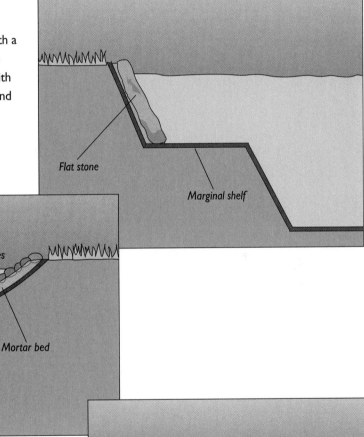

Flat stone

Marginal shelf

Medium-size stones

Mortar bed

Providing drainage
Before installing turf edging, dig a channel around the entire rim of the pool and fill it with gravel. This channel will collect any excess surface water. To prevent soil from draining into the pond, the trench should lead away from the pond at some point.

Drainage channel

Making Waterfalls

Building a waterfall is not as difficult as it might seem. The big concern is waterproofing. When it comes to esthetics, experimentation will reveal the most pleasing sights and sounds. **Where to build:** If you already have a sloping site next to the pond, much of the work—moving a large mound of earth to form the foundation of the falls—is already done. If you are building the pond and waterfall at the same time, the excavated earth can be used to create this mound. Remember that to ensure stability, the mound must be allowed to settle before it is wet down and tamped.

With this base in place, turn your imagination loose to create a design for the falls. Using a rake, draw a line in the mound of earth, extending from the pond to the top, where the header pool will be located. As with streams, twists and turns are easy to incorporate and will add a degree of authenticity to the waterfall.

The next step is to stake out and excavate the site as shown in the steps starting on the following page. Remember, to plan for any necessary plumbing *(page 158)*. And be sure that each small step over which the water will cascade is level from side to side. Note: The lowest pool

ANATOMY OF A WATERFALL

Shown below is a well-designed waterfall. The foundation can be the dirt excavated when you dug your pool, perhaps augmented by a retaining wall *(page 154)*. In this self-contained system, water is pumped from the main pond up to a moderately sized header pool. From there, it cascades down to the main pond. Rocks divert the water to separate the falls into two divergent paths, while edging rocks, properly placed and secured, with all gaps filled, prevent any water loss. The result is an interesting, moving water feature.

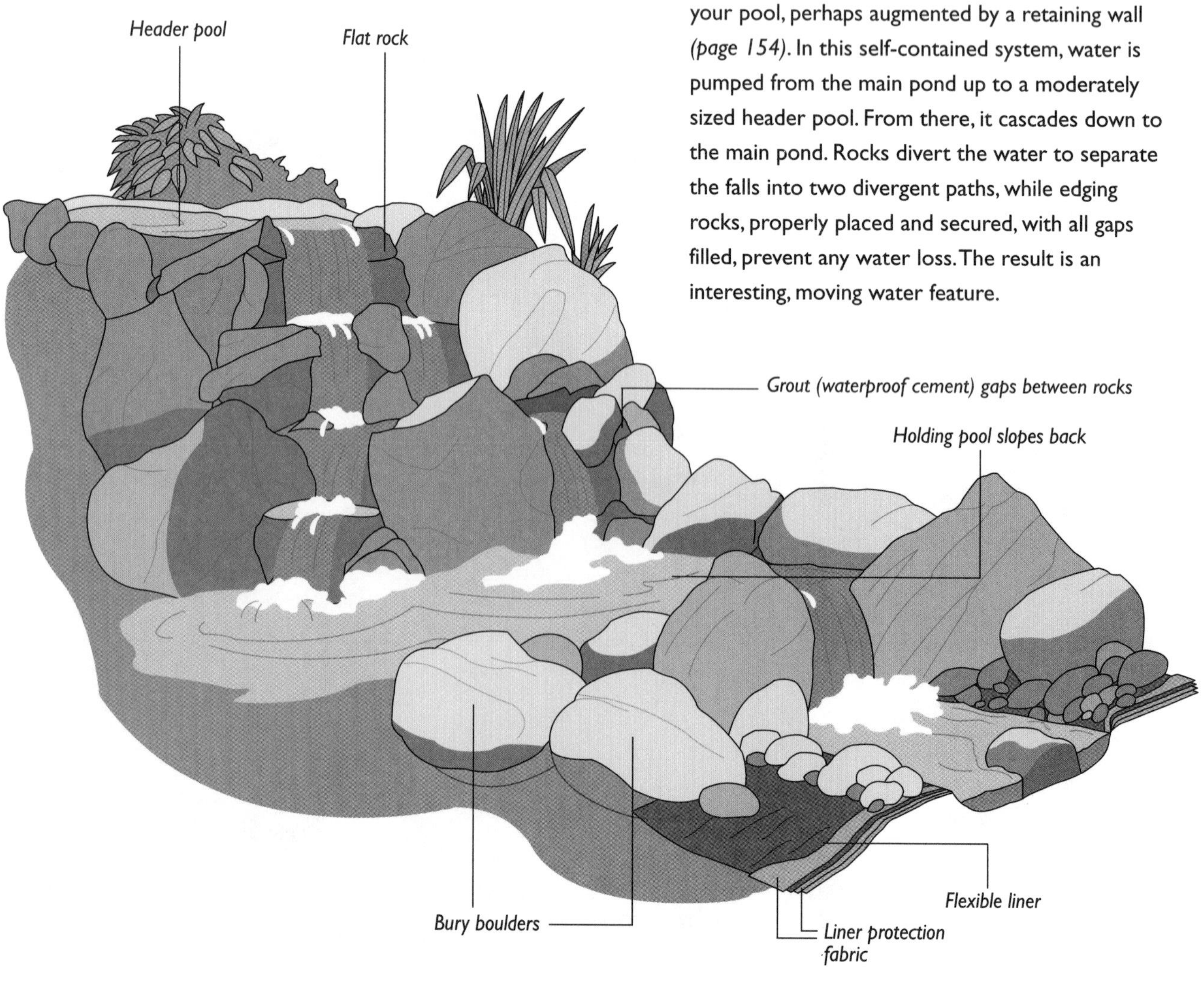

Header pool

Flat rock

Grout (waterproof cement) gaps between rocks

Holding pool slopes back

Bury boulders

Liner protection fabric

Flexible liner

must be large enough to hold all the water from the waterfall when the pump is turned off.

Materials: Waterfalls can be built with flexible liners, free-form concrete, or using preformed units *(page 155)*. For the home pond builder, flexible liners provide the best combination of design freedom and ease of installation. A liner can be sized to fit any waterfall you choose.

Because it will be protected from the sun's damaging rays beneath the waterfall, you have the flexibility of choosing a cheaper PVC variety. Where sharp rocks will be used, however, it is a good idea to lay protective material, such as sand or liner protection fabric, both under and over the liner to prevent puncturing.

Rocks and plants: The toughest part of building a waterfall is getting any big boulders in place. Position these rocks carefully to avoid displacing the liner. The rocks and plants you choose to include in and around the waterfall should match the plantings and rocks already in the garden. For the flat stones that will form the steps of the falls, you may need to go to a local stone dealer and carefully select rocks that fit your design.

Building a waterfall

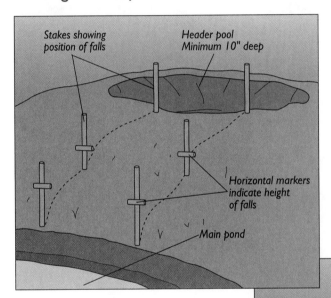

Stakes showing position of falls

Header pool Minimum 10" deep

Horizontal markers indicate height of falls

Main pond

1 Laying out the falls
Once you have prepared the site for the waterfall and decided on its course, lay out the path by driving in a pair of stakes at each step. In the example shown, width is uniform. If it is not in your example, indicate this with the stakes.

2 Excavating the site
Starting at the bottom of the mound, excavate the waterfall, using the stakes as guides. If the earth does not seem firm enough to hold the shape, allow it to settle further or tamp it again. Make the sides of the falls roughly vertical with each step approximately horizontal. At the top, create a header pool to house the inlet pipe from the pool and form the uppermost tier of the falls.

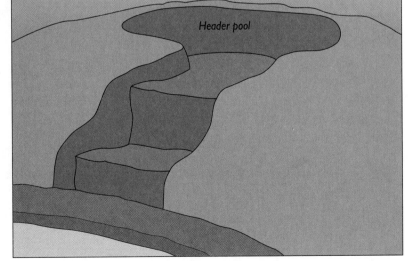

Header pool

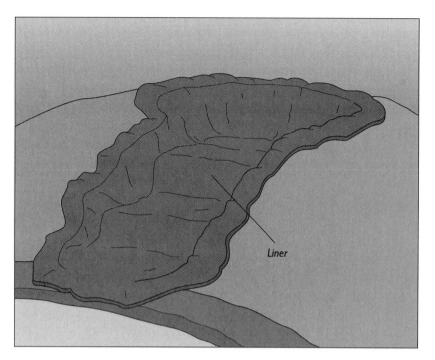

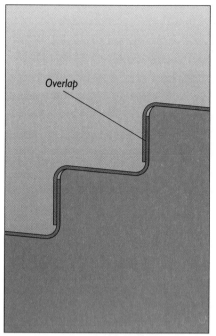

3 Installing the liner

Cut a piece of liner to fit over the entire waterfall with about a 12-inch overlap all around. Make sure that the waterfall liner and pond liner overlap. If you need to use more than one liner, make sure the pieces overlap at a fall and that the lower liner extends higher than the water in the fall *(above, right)*. With the liner in place, run water down the falls to check for leaks wherever the liner overlaps. It's a good idea to do this several times during construction.

4 Laying the flat stones

Lay the first flat stone on the bottom step of the falls so it overhangs the edge of the pool by 2 to 3 inches. Next, set a stone flat against the back of that step. These backing stones should be slightly higher than the rise of the steps. For added strength, add a bit of mortar between these stones. Lay the next flat stone horizontally on the next step so it overhangs the backing stone by 2 to 3 inches. Continue placing horizontal and backing stones in this manner to the top of the falls, laying the final rock flat in the bottom of the header pool.

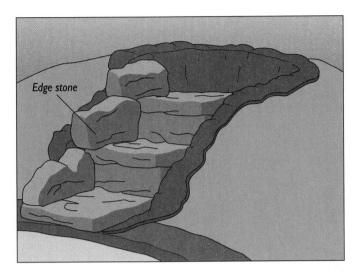

Edge stone

5 Placing edge rocks

Set an edge stone at each step along one side of the falls. These stones should be higher than the surrounding earth at the sides of the falls. Repeat this procedure along the other side of the falls and around the header pool. Lastly, mix a small amount of cement with a waterproofing agent and color to blend it with the rocks. Using a trowel or a paintbrush, spread the cement in the gaps between rocks to seal them and prevent water from running underneath.

Waterfall Options

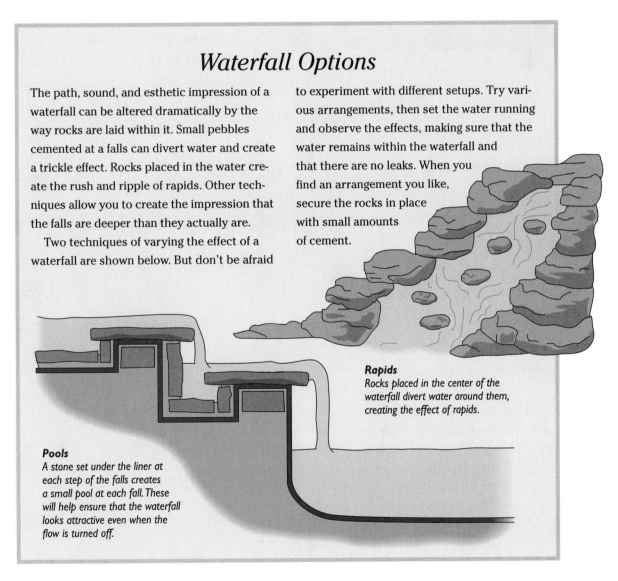

The path, sound, and esthetic impression of a waterfall can be altered dramatically by the way rocks are laid within it. Small pebbles cemented at a falls can divert water and create a trickle effect. Rocks placed in the water create the rush and ripple of rapids. Other techniques allow you to create the impression that the falls are deeper than they actually are.

Two techniques of varying the effect of a waterfall are shown below. But don't be afraid to experiment with different setups. Try various arrangements, then set the water running and observe the effects, making sure that the water remains within the waterfall and that there are no leaks. When you find an arrangement you like, secure the rocks in place with small amounts of cement.

Rapids
Rocks placed in the center of the waterfall divert water around them, creating the effect of rapids.

Pools
A stone set under the liner at each step of the falls creates a small pool at each fall. These will help ensure that the waterfall looks attractive even when the flow is turned off.

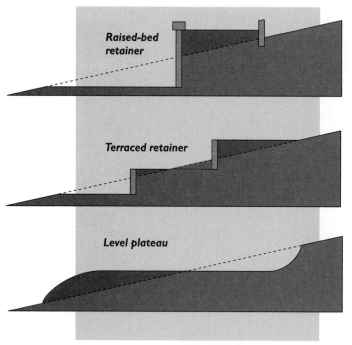

Raised-bed retainer

Terraced retainer

Level plateau

RETAINING WALL DESIGNS

Retaining walls are used to hold up a higher level of earth. Many pond builders find them suitable for the edges of a large pond or to create a waterfall on a naturally sloping site. The first task is preparing the slope. Three methods are shown at left. In the first, a raised bed is created by cutting away below the wall site and filling on the uphill side. The second technique divides the total wall height into two smaller walls, creating terraces. In the third, the slope is cut away and the earth moved downhill to create a plateau. Hardy, firm-rooted plants will also help retain the soil. It's best to plant right after the wall is done. Two types of wall construction are shown below.

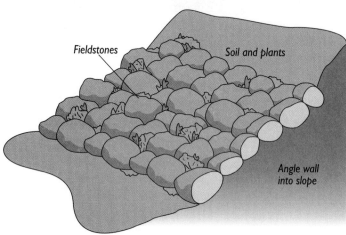

Fieldstones

Soil and plants

Angle wall into slope

TWO TYPES OF RETAINING WALLS

Properly grouted, reinforced concrete-block walls are an extremely strong, economical form of wall construction, small or large. In the example shown at right, the footing is cast first, then the wall is erected, using bond-beam blocks. Every other block in the lowest course is notched to receive plastic pipes for drainage. A mortar cap completes the project. Thick, mortared stone retaining walls (above) are strong and possess a rough-hewn beauty. They should be tilted back into the slope to increase holding power. The joints can be packed with earth and planted to enhance the wall's appearance.

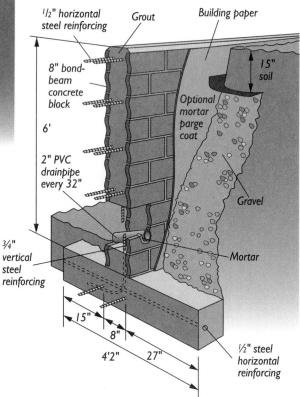

½" horizontal steel reinforcing

Grout

Building paper

8" bond-beam concrete block

6'

2" PVC drainpipe every 32"

15" soil

Optional mortar parge coat

Gravel

Mortar

¾" vertical steel reinforcing

15"

8"

4'2"

27"

½" steel horizontal reinforcing

154

Preformed units come in a wide range of styles to create various types and sizes of waterfalls and streams. They are available in different materials, including lightweight plastic, fiberglass, reconstituted stone, or concrete. Regardless of the manufacturer, the basic installation is the same. As with a natural waterfall, the first necessity is a mound of earth that has been well packed to support the units. Once plumbing lines are supplied, the units can be permanently laid and camouflaged with stones and plants.

With large models, add a liner underneath to prevent water loss from splashing. Use the steps below to guide you through the process.

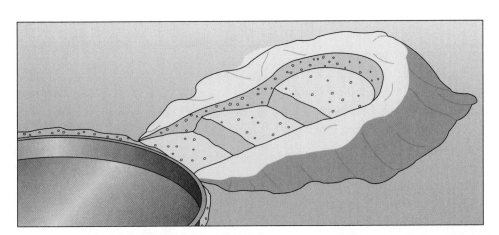

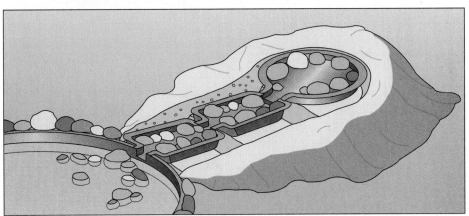

Installing preformed units
Excavate a mound of earth to fit the units roughly, building steps as for a handmade waterfall (above, top). Then, starting at the bottom, lay the units in place on the mound, arranging them as desired. Make sure they are level and that the lip of each unit overlaps the edge of the one below. Always check that the arrangement is satisfactory by running water from top to bottom with a hose. When you are satisfied with the flow of water, remove the units and, starting at the bottom, set them permanently.

Put a few blobs of cement on the bottom of the first unit and position it. Continue with the other units, checking for level as you go. When all the units are in place, set stones along the inside edges to secure them (above, bottom) and backfill around the units with damp soil or sand. Remember to install all necessary plumbing before backfilling. Add stones and plants beside the waterfall to conceal the units and finish the waterfall.

Building Streams

Streams share many construction details with waterfalls and pools. Most garden streams begin with a small falls and end in a holding pool. To plan a stream, lay out a hose or rope in the general course you want the stream to follow. If you are trying to create a design that mimics nature, include curves in your plan. The easiest method of building a stream is with a flexible liner, though concrete is occasionally used. The dry streambed is a classic Japanese design.

The information below should guide you through the stream-building process. No matter which design you choose, it's important to make the streambed level from side to side. The information on the following page should help you accomplish this goal. It will also show you how to incorporate plants into your stream.

Excavating a stream

Leveling from bank to bank

During excavation, build a T-shaped guide out of some scrap lumber: Its length should equal the depth of the streambed. Excavate the stream roughly to its finished depth, then check the banks for level, using a level and a straightedge as shown at right. When the proper depth is reached, insert a stake in the center of the bed at that point. Continue in this manner until the length of the stream is excavated.

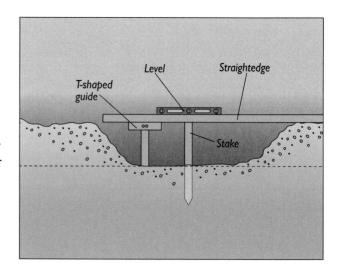

Planting a stream

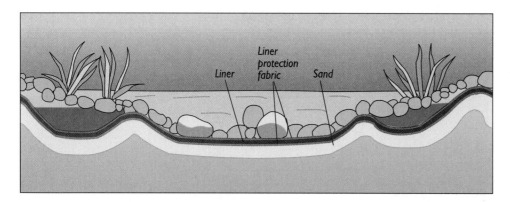

Hiding a stream liner

Plants enhance the appearance of a stream and add authenticity to a design. To allow for plants, dig shallow trenches on either side of the streambed when you are excavating. Extend the liner to cover these trenches and fill them with soil. Install marginal or moisture-loving plants, then cover the area with gravel or pebbles to prevent soil leakage.

STREAM CONSTRUCTION

Be sure that the proposed channel is able to handle the maximum flow from your pump, plus some additional natural runoff. For pump information, refer to pages 158-161. A finished depth of 3 to 7 inches works well; anything deeper than that requires a great deal of water. The slope should be mild. A series of steps—similar to those of a waterfall—joined by small, dammed cascades will keep water from running off too quickly and retain some of it when the pump is switched off. Experiment with rock placement in the finished stream to adjust the flow.

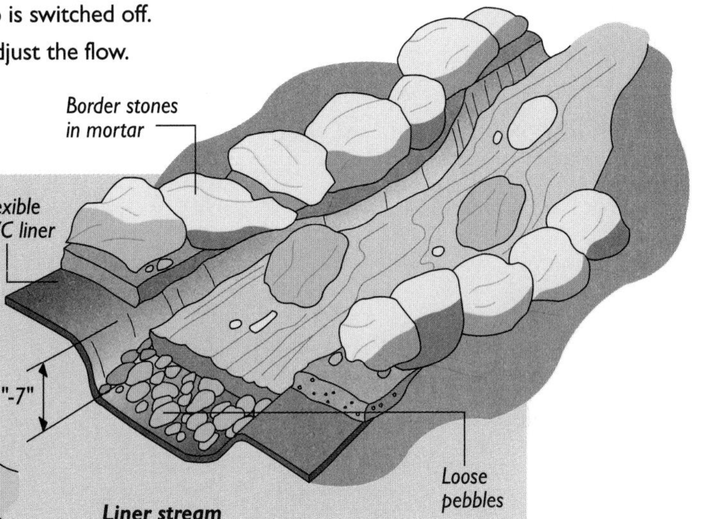

Border stones
in mortar

Flexible
PVC liner

Embedded
pebbles in
wet concrete

3"-7"

2" concrete

2" crushed rock

Gravel

Chicken wire

Loose
pebbles

Liner stream

Flexible liners may require some careful seamwork, but it's the quickest way to create a waterproof membrane. It's also easy to camouflage. Once the trench is excavated, the liner is simply laid in place and secured with border stones mortared in position.

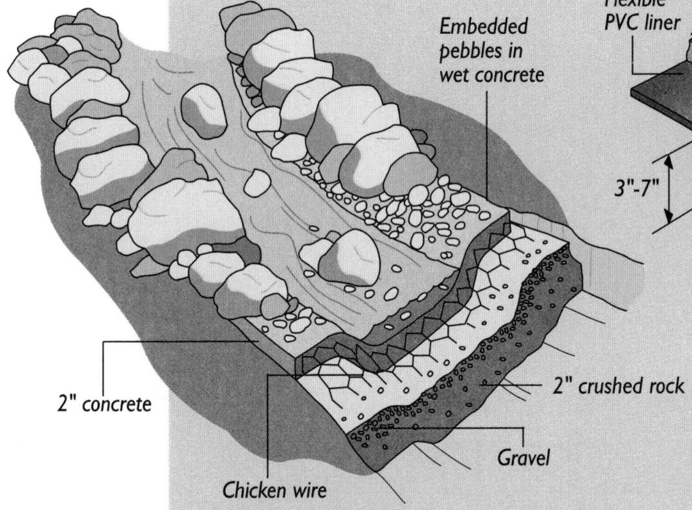

Concrete stream

A small channel will serve as a form for a concrete stream. Lay down 2" of ³/4" crushed rock, apply a layer of fine gravel, and cover with chicken wire. Pour 2" of concrete, working it into the base rocks or wire and troweling it up the sides. Roughen the surface with a stiff broom after it has started to harden.

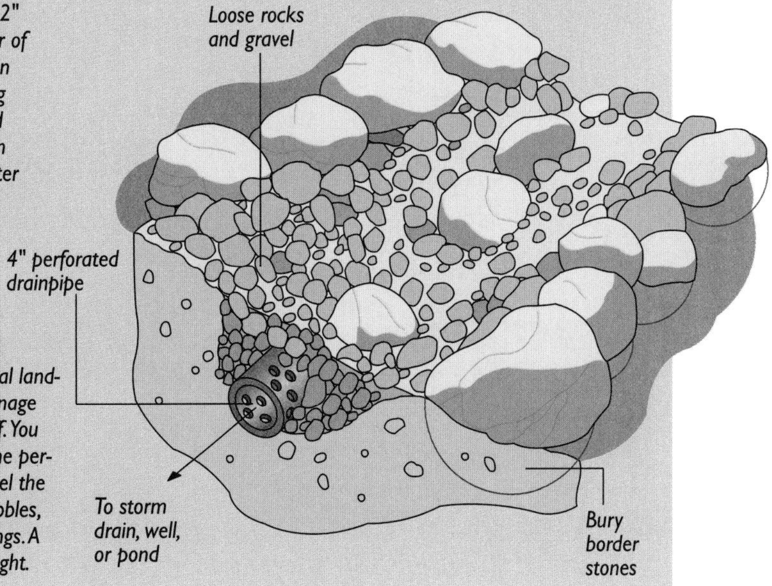

Loose rocks
and gravel

4" perforated
drainpipe

Dry streambed

The "dry streambed" is an effective option for a natural landscape, as well as for a drainage channel for seasonal runoff. You won't need a liner, just some perforated drainpipe to channel the water, mixed rocks and pebbles, and selected border plantings. A 2 percent grade is about right.

To storm
drain, well,
or pond

Bury
border
stones

Pond Plumbing

Although some pools don't require pumps—or call for only a small, submersible pump to drive a fountain jet—the vast majority of water gardens need pumps and a simple plumbing system. Fortunately, today's pumps and plumbing for garden pools are relatively easy for the do-it-yourselfer to install. The following pages contain information on pumps, pipes and fittings, valves and drains, and filters, along with a look at some sample plumbing systems. These will help you through the process of choosing and setting up the plumbing for your water garden.

Choosing a pump: The mechanical heart of a fountain or waterfall, a pump consists of a set of whirling blades through which the water passes and by which it is pressurized into further motion. A selection of pumps is shown on page 159. Submersible pumps greatly simplify plumbing. They sit on the floor of the pool, often hidden only by the water itself, and operate silently—an advantage over external pumps. Submersibles also tend to require less maintenance than external pumps, and don't need to be primed. Flexible tubing or rigid piping—generally, tubing is easier to work with—carries water to the

Calculating Pool Volume

Selecting a pump, a filter, water treatment, or fish medication all depend upon a working knowledge of your pool's capacity in gallons. To find a pool's volume, first calculate its area, which corresponds to the length times the width, then multiply the area by the average depth and a conversion factor (7.5). The trick is finding the "length and width" of a pool with an irregular shape. If you can't find a shape below that approximates your pool, divide the outline into units of simpler shapes, figure the volume of each chunk, and then add them together for the total.

Area: square feet of surface
Volume: gallons of water

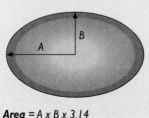

Area = A x B x 3.14
Volume = area x average depth x 7.5

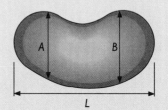

Area = (A + B) x L x 0.45 (approx.)
Volume = area x average depth x 7.5

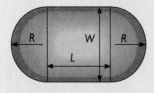

Area = (L x W) + (R x R x 3.14)
Volume = area x average depth x 7.5

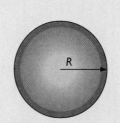

Area = R x R x 3.14
Volume = area x average depth x 7.5

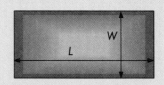

Area = L x W
Volume = area x average depth x 7.5

fountain or waterfall or simply circulates the water back into the pond.

Choosing the right size: All manufacturers give electrical specifications—amps, horsepower—for their products, which are important because they measure how much electricity—watts—will be used to do the job. But the practical measure of a pump's performance is the volume of water it will pump vertically, telling you how many gallons an hour a pump can deliver at a given height, also known as the head.

Fountain spray jets are usually designed for a specific pressure,

A PANOPLY OF PUMPS

There are literally hundreds of pumps on the market today. Dealers usually have knowledgeable staff on hand to advise you on which model will fulfill the needs of your water feature. Whatever type of pump you choose, it should be sturdy and able both to run continuously and be taken apart for routine maintenance. The gallery of pumps below will provide you with some options.

Nonsubmersible, or recirculating, pump
Surface pump capable of running large water features.

Submersible pump
Placed in pond; suitable for running small fountains and waterfalls.

Fountain pump
Submersible pump with prefit attachment for small water fountain.

Pool pump
Powerful submersible pump, useful for running or draining large water features.

Circulator pump
Surface pump that moves high volume of water at low pressure. Should be kept sheltered from elements.

PIPES AND FITTINGS

The selection of pipes and fittings shown at right can be purchased at plumbing, pond, or aquarium supply stores. Bring a plan of your system with you and consult with the supplier for the most cost-efficient, effective setup.

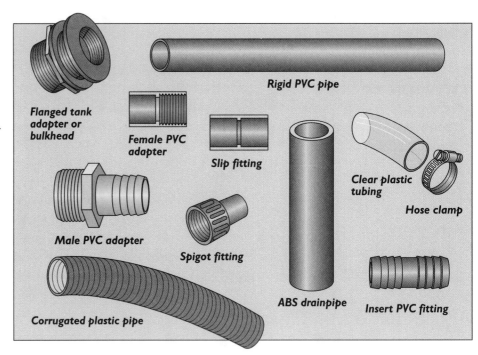

Flanged tank adapter or bulkhead

Female PVC adapter

Slip fitting

Rigid PVC pipe

Clear plastic tubing

Hose clamp

Male PVC adapter

Spigot fitting

ABS drainpipe

Insert PVC fitting

Corrugated plastic pipe

PVC gate valve

Gate valve

Check valves

Ball valve

3-way valve

Main drain

Bottom drain

Float valve

Check valve

VALVES AND DRAINS

A gate valve is handy for simple on/off use and for isolating a pump, filter, or drain line. To control flow, opt for a ball valve. A 3-way valve allows you to shut off the water, send a controlled flow to a fountain head, or open up a line for draining the pool. Check valves keep water flowing in one direction, maintaining a pump's prime and preventing backflow. Drains come in a variety of shapes and sizes and are usually available at spa and swimming pool suppliers. They need some kind of cap or screen to keep leaves and debris out. Special flanged fittings or bulkheads—such as the one illustrated in the pipes and fittings inventory at the top of the page—are made for liners and fiberglass shells to ensure a tight seal where the drain or pipe has penetrated the liner or shell.

but waterfalls and streams are more a question of choice. To choose a pump for a small water feature, measure the vertical distance from the water level to the top of the stream or waterfall. Then, using a garden hose, start a flow of water from the top that approximates the volume of water you want. Collect this water in a 5-gallon bucket for one minute, then multiply the results to get gallons per hour. Compare that figure with the manufacturer's performance data.

When sizing a pump for a large system, it's best to hook up a temporary pump to a 1½-inch hose or the finished plumbing. Your pump should be able to recycle an adequate flow to any filter system, so take this into account as well.

Locating your pump: In most cases, install the pump to keep the distance it has to move the water as short as possible. For example,

a waterfall pump is usually situated right at the base of the falls. The one exception is when the pump's primary function is to drive a filter: In this case, consider positioning the intake pipe—and the pump itself—at the opposite end of the pool for maximum circulation.

Elevate a submersible pump on bricks at the bottom of the pool to keep it free from silt and other pool debris. Alternatively, you may wish to form a small gravel-lined pump vault at the bottom of the pool, covering the opening with removable wire mesh. Always place some type of strainer in front of the pump to filter dirt and leaves. (Many pumps include a built-in pre-filter, which blocks large debris at the pump intake.) Ideally, a recirculating pump should be housed in a lidded 3-foot by 5-foot cover—cast in concrete or built from wood. You can cam-

ouflage the vault with plants or hide it behind a retaining wall. Before placing your pump, consider how you will supply electricity to power it *(page 166)*

Pipes and fittings: The illustrations on page 160 represent a sampling of pipes and fittings that allow you to change direction, join pipe runs, and change from a screw-on fitting to a push-in fitting. Pipes and fittings for garden pool pumps should be plastic or galvanized steel, although on a small pump, rubber or clear plastic tubing can be used.

Whenever possible, choose plastic pipe and fittings for both water supply and drain lines: Plastic is easy to cut, straightforward to assemble, and won't corrode like copper or galvanized. Rigid Schedule 40 PVC is the standard, though flexible PVC, available in many areas, fits around difficult corners without fittings.

Installing a float valve

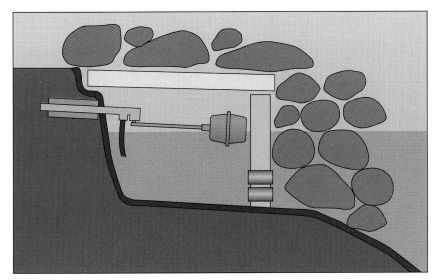

A float valve will automatically top up water lost to evaporation and splash. You'll need access to a nearby cold water pipe plus a fitting or two to make the hookup. A float valve can be located in the holding pool of a wall fountain, a niche in a pool's rock edging, or a separate, lidded chamber located near the main pool and concealed with rocks or plants, as shown at left.

ABS plastic can be substituted for PVC for larger drain lines. Consider 1½-inch pipe and fittings the norm for garden pool systems; large volumes of water may require 2-inch lines. Solvent fittings can be used for PVC connections in your plumbing system, but there is no need to go to the trouble: Threaded fittings and push-in, or compression, fittings will usually do the trick. To ensure that screw fittings are watertight, first wind pipe-wrap tape around the threads of the pipe.

Valves and drains: Valves allow you to control the flow of water to a fountain or waterfall, divert water to a nearby drain, or shut the entire system down for repairs or maintenance. Drains will not be needed in every pool. In a small pool or fountain, a submersible pump can double as a sump pump for draining. Larger pools should have a main drain to allow the pool to be drained for maintenance. Refer to the inventory on page 160.

Filters: In theory, a pool properly stocked with plant and animal life should not require any filtering device. In practice, overfeeding fish, excessive light, soil, and fish waste make a filter necessary. Also, pools with no plants will need some kind of filter to eliminate algae.

There are two types of filters commonly used by water gardeners: biological *(see opposite)* and mechanical. The latter work like strainers, stopping matter larger than their pore size from reentering the pond. They range from sand filters to cartridge filters. While they catch debris, mechanical filters do not purify the water. Hence they are often used in conjunction with a biological filter. A selection of filters is illustrated below.

FILTERS

As with pumps, there are many makes of filter on the market. Speak to a qualified dealer to find the model that will best fill your needs. Check to be sure that it can be cleaned easily.

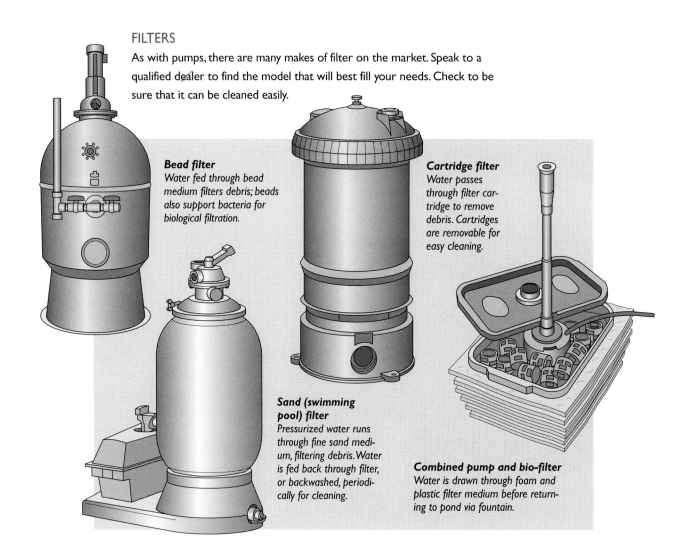

Bead filter
Water fed through bead medium filters debris; beads also support bacteria for biological filtration.

Cartridge filter
Water passes through filter cartridge to remove debris. Cartridges are removable for easy cleaning.

Sand (swimming pool) filter
Pressurized water runs through fine sand medium, filtering debris. Water is fed back through filter, or backwashed, periodically for cleaning.

Combined pump and bio-filter
Water is drawn through foam and plastic filter medium before returning to pond via fountain.

Biological Filters

Biological filters use bacteria to convert ammonia and nitrites in the pool water to nitrates and thus continue the purifying nitrogen cycle *(see page 106)*. The key to designing a biological system is creating a sand, gravel, or synthetic medium bed that the bacteria can call home, and pumping a steady flow of pool water through the filter medium with a constantly operating pump.

Location: You can situate a biological filter at the bottom of a water garden or in a remote location, connected by intake and outlet pipes. While the remote tank is easier to maintain, it also requires extra space and expense.

Large, deep, fiberglass shells are easy to retrofit for the in-pool version. Fiberglass is the typical solution for a remote holding tank since it's easy to set up and drill for fittings. Even plastic industrial drums will work well as filters.

Design: The biological filter is a 12- to 24-inch-deep media bed with an open space below, allowing the water to enter and exit at a leisurely pace. Water can travel up or down through the filter bed. Both upflow and downflow filters are shown below. Coarse aquarium sand is a traditional choice, though it is often replaced or accompanied by fiber padding and other media.

Ideally, the larger the filter the better, but a smaller version will work if it is well maintained. It takes up to 8 weeks for a bacterial colony to grow, but you can speed the process by seeding the filter from an existing medium.

Pump and hardware: Garden pool designers figure that the pump should turn over 1 to 2 gallons per minute per square foot of filter bed surface. That means that a 3- by 6-foot biological filter will require 18 to 36 gallons per minute, or 1,080 to 2,160 gallons per hour. A recirculating pump is best, as the filter must operate 24 hours a day or risk killing the bacteria that make it work.

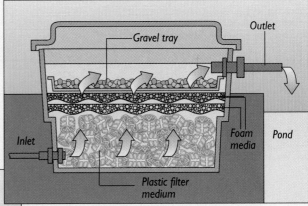

Upflow biological filter
Water flows upward through the plastic biological filter medium for biological filtration, then undergoes fine filtration of solids in the foam layers. Gravel prevents the foam from being pushed upward and provides another level of mechanical and biological filtration. Gravel tray and foam are removed for cleaning.

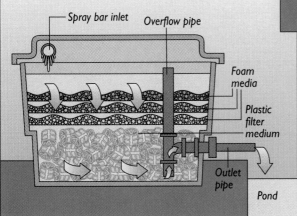

Downflow biological filter
Water enters through spray bar at the top of the filter and flows downward, receiving biological and mechanical filtration in the successively finer layers of foam and the bed of plastic filter medium below. A built-in overflow ensures that when the filter is blocked, water bypasses it. Foam is removable for cleaning.

Sample Plumbing Designs

Two-tiered wall fountain

A submersible pump elevated on bricks supplies two levels of a wall, or spill, fountain. Cover the pipe ends with decorative nozzles or figurines, or hide them between masonry units, leaving a narrow slot in mortar or grout. A three-way valve connects to a storm drain, allowing the pool to be drained for cleaning and other maintenance. A float valve is concealed in a separate chamber to refill the pool automatically when the water level dips below normal.

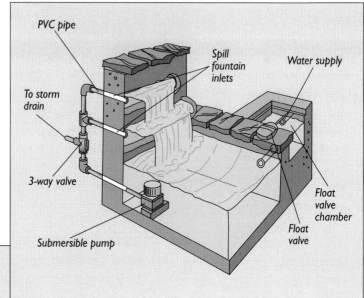

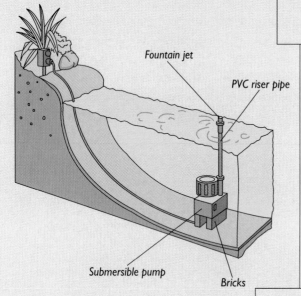

Small fountain

A submersible pump elevated on bricks with PVC riser pipe and a fountain attachment supply a simple spray fountain. An electrical outlet located beside the pond is concealed with plants and rock edgings.

Small waterfall

A submersible pump elevated on bricks and clear plastic tubing feeds a small pondside waterfall. An overflow pipe leading to a gravel border drain with 4" perforated drainpipe prevents water level from rising above the sides of the pond.

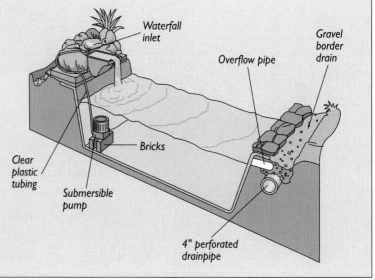

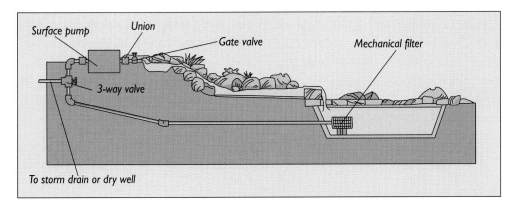

Small stream

A surface pump circulates water from a pond to the top of a stream. A mechanical filter catches debris at the intake. A three-way valve allows the system to be shut down and the pond to be drained for maintenance.

Large waterfall

Surface pump circulates water over waterfall. Check valve on pipeline between pond and pump prevents backflow. Drain allows pond to be emptied for maintenance or cleaning.

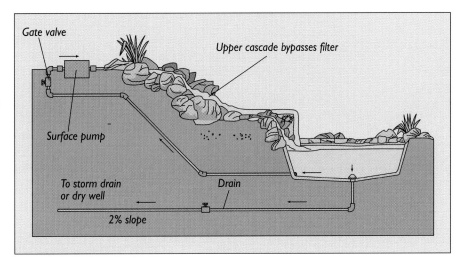

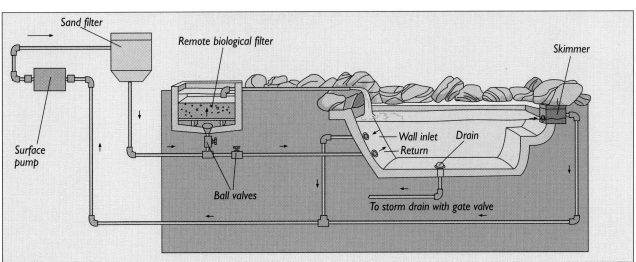

Koi pond with pressurized sand filter and biological filter

Surface pump circulates water from pool through pressurized sand filter for solid filtration. Ball valve allows some water to be diverted through upflow biological filter to waterfall. A surface skimmer, connected to the pump intake, pulls dirt, pollen, floating algae, and leaves into the filtration system. The skimmer is most effective when located on the downwind side of the pool; the wind helps the pump by pushing debris toward the opening. The drain allows pond to be emptied for maintenance.

Wiring and Lighting

For powering a pump, accenting plants and fish with lights, or illuminating paths with attractive outdoor fixtures, electricity is necessity for the garden pond. You can either extend your home's 120-volt system into the garden, or you can step the system down to 12 volts and use lighter-weight fixtures that can be easily moved.

A 12-volt installation (*page168*) is simple: Cable can lie on top of the ground, perhaps hidden by foliage, or in a narrow trench (with low-voltage wiring, there is much less danger that people or pets will suffer a harmful shock). In most areas, no electrical permit is

OUTDOOR FIXTURES

There is a wide choice of outdoor lights for the water garden. Regardless of what you choose, you'll want to avoid glare. An opaque covering on a fixture will create a warm glow rather than a hot spot of light. You can also use lower light levels. At night, a little light goes a long way: 20 watts is considered "strong."

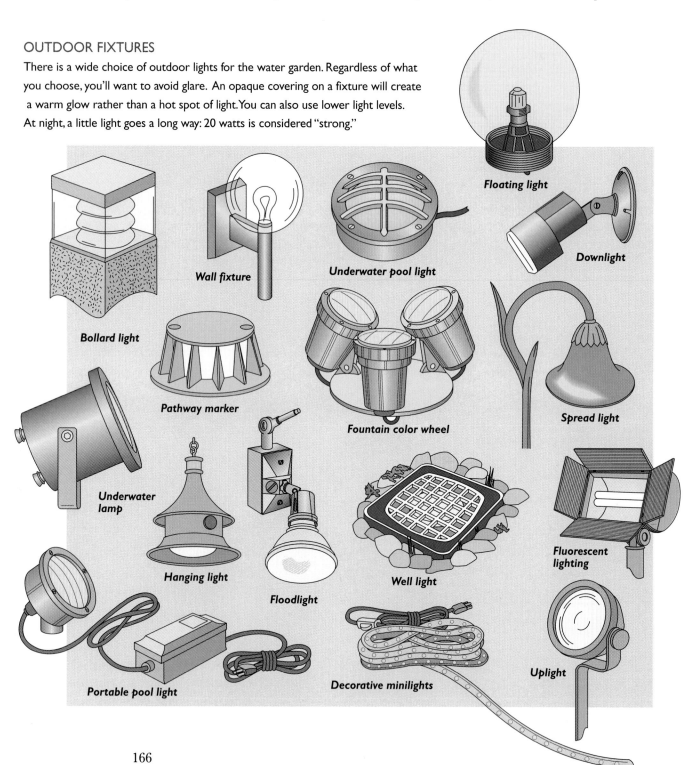

Floating light

Wall fixture

Underwater pool light

Downlight

Bollard light

Pathway marker

Fountain color wheel

Spread light

Underwater lamp

Hanging light

Floodlight

Well light

Fluorescent lighting

Portable pool light

Decorative minilights

Uplight

required for installing a system that extends from a low-voltage plug-in transformer (the most common kind).

For brighter lighting, pumps, and other pool accessories, 120-volt wiring *(page 169)* packs a bigger punch—and requires both buried cable and an electrical permit. Code restrictions are particularly strict for installations near to and in the pool. If you are planning a 220-volt installation for a heavy-duty recirculating pump, you will need to hire a professional.

Before adding on to an existing circuit, it's smart to add up the watts marked on the bulbs and

GFCI

According to present electrical codes, any new outside receptacle must be protected by a ground fault circuit interrupter (GFCI or GFI). Whenever the amounts of incoming and outgoing current are not equal—indicating current leakage (a "ground fault")—the GFCI opens the circuit instantly, cutting off the power. To install a GFCI, make the connections with plastic wire nuts, following this sequence: 1. Turn off the circuit; 2. Strip 1 inch of insulation from the wire ends and twist the ends clockwise $1^{1}/_{2}$ turns; 3. Snip $^{3}/_{8}$" to $^{1}/_{2}$" off the twisted wires; 4. Screw the wire nut clockwise on the wires. Twist a short "jumper" wire from the box's grounding screw together with the other two grounding wires. If this is the end of the run, snip off the remaining outgoing wires from the GFCI and cover them with wire nuts as shown. The illustrations below will give you guidelines for installing a GFCI.

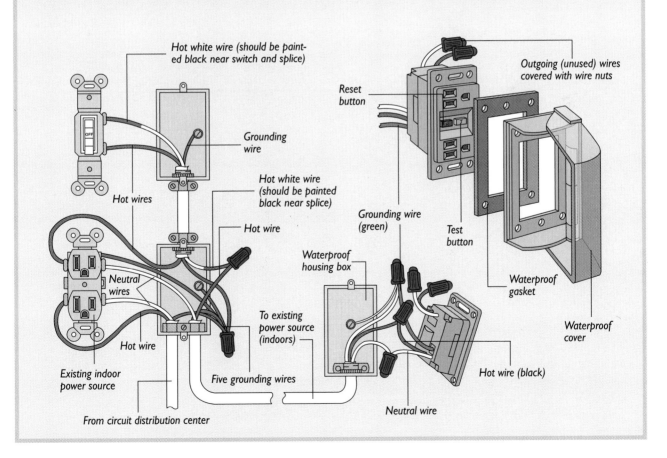

Hot white wire (should be painted black near switch and splice)

Reset button

Outgoing (unused) wires covered with wire nuts

Grounding wire

Hot white wire (should be painted black near splice)

Hot wires

Hot wire

Neutral wires

Waterproof housing box

Grounding wire (green)

Test button

Waterproof gasket

Hot wire

To existing power source (indoors)

Waterproof cover

Existing indoor power source

Five grounding wires

Hot wire (black)

From circuit distribution center

Neutral wire

appliances fed by that circuit. A 15-amp circuit, for example, can handle a continuous load of 1440 watts; a 20-amp circuit is rated for 1920 watts. The number of watts you can add is the difference between these figures and the total load already present on the circuit.

When purchasing light fixtures for installation above water, be sure to get weather-resistant UL-approved materials. Aluminum, brass, copper, stainless steel, hard-finish plastics, or ceramic clays are all good choices.

There is one cardinal rule for the do-it-yourself electrician that stands above all: *Never work on any "live" circuit fixture, receptacle, or switch.* Your life may very well depend on it. If fuses protect your circuits, remove the appro-priate fuse and take it with you. In a panel or subpanel equipped with circuit breakers, switch the appro-priate breaker to the OFF position to disconnect the circuit. For an extra measure of safety, tape over the switch.

If you need help to add a new cir-cuit or you have any doubts about how to hook up to an existing one, consult an electrician.

Adding a 12-Volt System

To install a low-voltage system for outdoor use, you'll need a trans-former, usually housed in a water-proof box, to step the household current of 120 volts down to 12 volts. Mount the transformer near the watertight switch or receptacle and then run a cable a few inches below the ground from the low-voltage side of the transformer to the desired locations for your

lights. Some fixtures simply clip onto the wire, while others must be wired into the system. Some low-voltage lights come in a kit with a transformer. Be sure to use the right size of wire given in the instructions. Most low-voltage out-door fixtures use stranded wire cable, the size of the wires in the cable depending on the aggregate wattage of the fixtures to be

served. Here are the appropriate sizes for some typical wattages:

#14 wire: up to 144 watts at 12 volts
#12 wire: up to 192 watts at 12 volts
#10 wire: up to 288 watts at 12 volts

If you don't have an outlet to plug the transformer into, have an elec-trician install a GFCI outlet, or install one yourself (page 167).

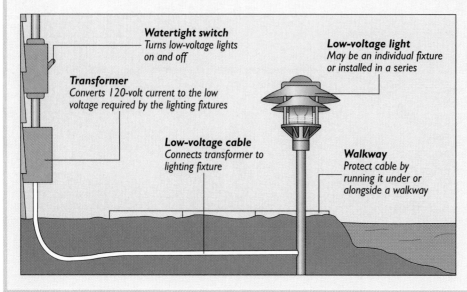

Watertight switch
Turns low-voltage lights on and off

Transformer
Converts 120-volt current to the low voltage required by the lighting fixtures

Low-voltage cable
Connects transformer to lighting fixture

Low-voltage light
May be an individual fixture or installed in a series

Walkway
Protect cable by running it under or alongside a walkway

A typical 12-volt installation
Since a 12-volt system uses a greatly reduced voltage, special conduit and boxes of other out-door wiring are not required. Most transformers are rated for home use from 100 to 300 watts. The higher the rating, the more lengths of 100-foot cable—and consequently the more light fix-tures—can be connected to the transformer. Most transformers are encased in watertight boxes; to be safe, though, plan to install yours at least a foot off the ground in a sheltered location.

Setting Up a 120-Volt System

A 120-volt outdoor lighting system offers several advantages. For starters, a light from a single fixture can illuminate a larger area—especially useful for security and for lighting trees from the ground. In addition, it offers flexibility: not only light fixtures, but electric garden tools can be plugged into 120-volt outdoor outlets.

A 120-volt outdoor system consists of a set of fixtures and some underground 120-volt cable or conduit. The length used depends on the size of the wire. Your electrician will probably connect the system through an indoor switch and timer to an existing electrical source, as shown below at right. This will allow you to turn lights on and off by hand or let the timer do it for you.

The diagrams shown below will help you understand the basics of installing a 120-volt system. But unless you are well versed in all aspects of electricity, leave the job to a professional. If you do the work yourself, remember to shut off the power first.

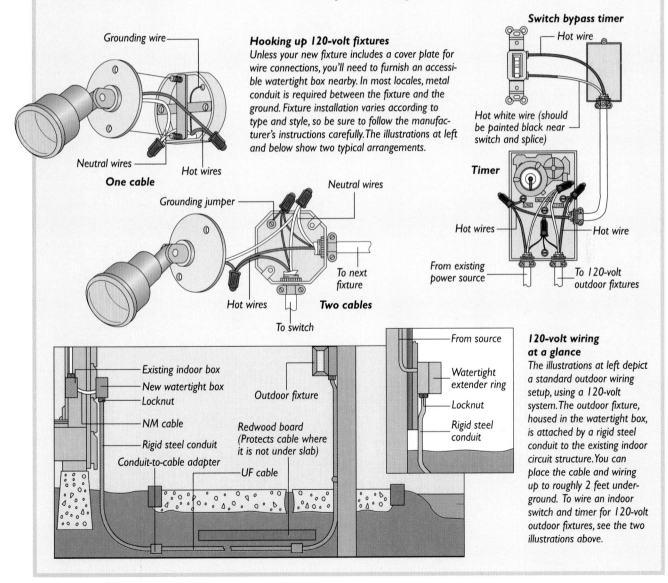

Grounding wire

Neutral wires

Hot wires

One cable

Hooking up 120-volt fixtures
Unless your new fixture includes a cover plate for wire connections, you'll need to furnish an accessible watertight box nearby. In most locales, metal conduit is required between the fixture and the ground. Fixture installation varies according to type and style, so be sure to follow the manufacturer's instructions carefully. The illustrations at left and below show two typical arrangements.

Grounding jumper

Neutral wires

Hot wires

To next fixture

To switch

Two cables

Switch bypass timer

Hot wire

Hot white wire (should be painted black near switch and splice)

Timer

Hot wires

Hot wire

From existing power source

To 120-volt outdoor fixtures

Existing indoor box
New watertight box
Locknut
NM cable
Rigid steel conduit
Conduit-to-cable adapter

Outdoor fixture

Redwood board (Protects cable where it is not under slab)

UF cable

From source

Watertight extender ring

Locknut

Rigid steel conduit

120-volt wiring at a glance
The illustrations at left depict a standard outdoor wiring setup, using a 120-volt system. The outdoor fixture, housed in the watertight box, is attached by a rigid steel conduit to the existing indoor circuit structure. You can place the cable and wiring up to roughly 2 feet underground. To wire an indoor switch and timer for 120-volt outdoor fixtures, see the two illustrations above.

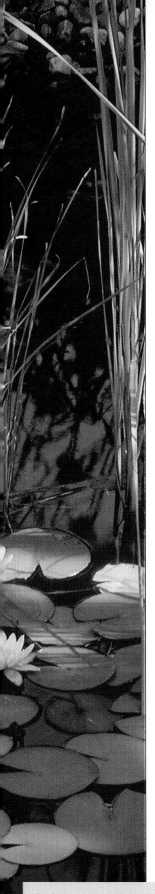

Water
GARDEN
MAINTENANCE

With your garden pool installed and planted, you will want to embark on a careful maintenance program to keep it in top shape. If your pool is well built, structural maintenance should be minimal. Plants, fish, and water are another matter. All require some regular care to keep the pond flourishing.

The following chapter contains all the information you will need to maintain a healthy water garden, from sections on seasonal care, cleaning, and pond repairs to information on keeping fish and plants over the winter and dealing with pests and illnesses when they threaten your pond's inhabitants. The section on water chemistry will help you win the battle with the most persistent pond maintenance problem: algae. Finally, the chapter contains important pond safety guidelines as well as a useful listing of suppliers, clubs, and associations where you can purchase materials and share your love of water gardening with others.

By following a regular maintenance schedule throughout the year, pond owners help ensure clean, clear water and vibrant plant life, the hallmarks of a healthy water garden.

A Season-by-Season Guide

All gardens require periodic maintenance, and water gardens are no exception. Regular care will ensure that everything stays in balance and the pond functions normally. Maintenance work can be roughly divided by season, although there is some overlap. Think of it as preventive medicine for the garden. It will help you avoid larger problems down the road, and ensure that you will catch anything that does go wrong early enough to fix it without breaking your back—or emptying your bank account.

Most gardens are installed in the spring, so that is the logical starting point to begin our discussion.

Spring: Whether it is a brand-new installation or a decade-old pond, in spring, the water garden returns to life. Begin by inspecting the pool and edgings for damage caused by freezing or frost. Make any necessary repairs as soon as weather permits. If your pond is stocked with fish, they will have begun moving, but much more slowly than in summer. Fish need heat for proper digestion, so feed them around noon hour. Pond protection devices such as cover nets should be left in place until marginal plants grow up around the edges of the water garden to shelter the more lethargic fish from predators. Once the marginals start to sprout, trim all dead foliage from them. If the pond contains much debris in the form of dead leaves or other similar matter, remove whatever amount you can and make a partial water change *(page 178)* to give the pond a fresh start for the season.

If you are considering making design changes to the pond, now is the time to do the work. The soft ground will make any excavation relatively easy to carry out, and the new installation will have plenty of time to mature.

If you have turned off the pump over the winter, clean it thoroughly before restarting, Also clean and reinstall any filters that you took in over the winter. To get biological filters functioning at full power again, consider purchasing starter bacterial cultures from a pond supply store. Lastly, check the condition of all electrical wiring and equipment and replace any damaged components.

Summer: When it comes to plant and animal life, as well as pool maintenance, summer is the season of activity in the water garden. Plants will be in bloom and fish at full activity. Keep an eye on the algae level in the water. String algae should be removed regularly by hand. If the water appears green for an extended period of time, a biological filter might be in order. As the pond will be at full activity, it is especially important to keep existing strainers and filters clean.

If you plan to add new plants, particularly tropicals, or fish, summer is the best time. It is also the right season to divide mature marginal plants *(page 87)*. This will encourage fresh, healthy growth. In summer, female fish will begin to spawn. Ensure that you have a good amount of plant life on the bottom of the pond to protect young fry from larger fish. During the heat of the summer, diseases and parasites affecting both plants and fish are also at their peak. Monitor all pond life carefully and use an appropriate treatment as soon you diagnose a problem *(page 182)*. The hotter summer weather will also cause water to evaporate more quickly and oxygen levels to drop. Monitor water level and top up the pond as necessary.

Finally, late summer is the best time for a full-fledged pond cleaning *(page 174)*. If your pond is reasonably well maintained, however, this procedure will only be needed every few years.

Autumn: With the gardening season winding down, it is time to enjoy the final blooms and color of the season, and prepare the pond for the upcoming winter. To prevent leaves from falling in the water, install a protective net over the pond and remove them regularly. Trim all dead or dying plant life and remove any plants that seem diseased. Marginals should be trimmed after the first frost. Do not cut them below the water level—this causes death in some species. Oxygenators that have reached the surface of the pond should be cut back to prevent them from being frozen into the ice. Any plants that are less hardy should be lowered into deeper water.

Early autumn is perfect for planting and dividing bog plants, which are best handled outside their growing season. All other planting is best avoided during this season.

Monitor fish very closely for parasites or disease as it is next to impossible to treat them for problems in winter. Also, as the weather gets colder, limit feeding to the warmest days. If you plan to allow the fish to winter in the pool, choose a method of preventing the water from freezing over completely *(page 185)*.

Winter: Depending on the location of the pond, winter can be anything from icy cold to relatively balmy.

When the temperature drops below 40 degrees, fish enter partial hibernation. Provided the pool is deep enough, extreme cold will not kill fish, but it is crucial to maintain some area of ice-free water.

Prop a submersible pump well off the bottom of the pond so it does not disturb the fish. Turn it on periodically through the winter to keep it in good running condition. If the pump will be turned off, remove it from the pond. Surface pumps must be drained and then insulated to prevent damage. Unless you have valuable fish, don't run a biological filter. Simply drain the filter and disconnect it from the system. The season-by-season chart below will provide you with a guide to keeping the pond in shape throughout the year.

MAINTENANCE CHART

	POND	PLANTS	ANIMALS	EQUIPMENT
Spring	Inspect liner, shell or concrete for holes or damaged areas and make necessary repairs. Scoop out dead leaves and debris. Make any desired design changes.	Trim dead foliage from plants. Remove protective netting once marginals have come up.	Start feeding fish, waiting until the warmer afternoon temperatures. Inspect fish for disease or parasites.	Clean and reinstall any pumps and filters taken off line over winter. Inspect electrical components and replace damaged equipment.
Summer	If needed, clean the pond. Remove string algae by hand; monitor water condition. Monitor water level and top up as needed.	Add new plants, if desired. Perform root division on mature marginals. Trim dead blooms. Remove unwanted weeds.	Carefully monitor fish for illness. During spawning season, isolate female fish being attacked by spawning males.	Clean pump, strainer, and filter, as needed. Install filter if the pond suffers persistent poor water quality.
Autumn	Install protective net to prevent leaves from falling in pond. Inspect pond and make any necessary repairs before winter.	Trim dead plant life. Trim tops of oxygenators which have reached top of pond. Divide bog plants.	Inspect fish regularly for disease or parasites and treat immediately. Limit feeding to warmest days.	Clean pump, strainer, and filter, if required.
Winter	Turn off moving water features such as fountains or waterfalls.	Lower less hardy plants into water at least 9 inches deep. Bring tropicals inside.	Install heater to prevent pond from freezing over.	Prop submersible pumps off bottom. Drain and insulate unused pumps and filters.

Draining and Cleaning the Water Garden

Although a properly balanced pool should keep itself in working condition for long periods at a stretch, an occasional draining and cleaning may be required. Late summer or early fall are generally considered the best times for a pool-cleaning project. If you've installed a main drain, it's easy to empty the pool; otherwise, drain it with a pump, or use a hose as a siphon to drain the water to a large container in a nearby low-lying area. Remove any plants, bottom sediment, and leaves, being careful not to damage a liner or shell.

If you have fish, remove them from the pool. Drain about half of the water, then net the fish and move them to a shaded fiberglass holding tank, a large aquarium, or a large plastic garbage can filled with water. Shade the temporary container and, if possible, add some aeration in the form of a pool pump or at least a small aquarium air pump with airstone.

Inspect the pool shell or liner, especially if you suspect leaks. This is the time to correct any problems *(see pages 179-180)*.

To clean pool walls and bottom, spray them with a strong jet from the garden hose, then drain the pool once or twice more before refilling. Always use restraint when cleaning. Strong scrubbing can remove all beneficial bacteria from the pool.

Refurbishing a concrete garden pool is a little more involved. First drain the pool, then scrub the sides (including any tile) and bottom with a pool brush dipped in a solution of one part muriatic acid and one part water. You may need a hand brush or scouring pad to remove stubborn stains. Be sure to wear rubber gloves and eye protection when you are working—acid is caustic. Rinse the pool with a strong jet from the garden hose and let it dry for one to two days; then wash it again with a solution of trisodium phosphate (dissolve according to label instructions). Rinse again with water and allow the pool to dry overnight.

POOL CLEANING TOOLS

Draining and cleaning the water garden requires little more than a few simple tools and some elbow grease. The equipment shown at right should be available at most pond supply stores.

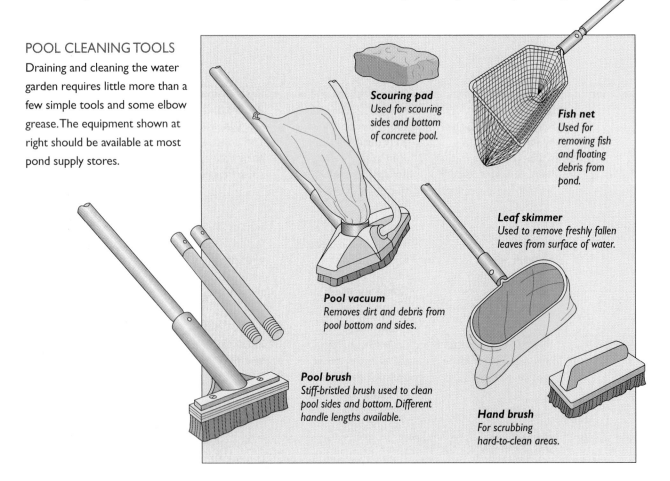

Scouring pad
Used for scouring sides and bottom of concrete pool.

Fish net
Used for removing fish and floating debris from pond.

Leaf skimmer
Used to remove freshly fallen leaves from surface of water.

Pool vacuum
Removes dirt and debris from pool bottom and sides.

Pool brush
Stiff-bristled brush used to clean pool sides and bottom. Different handle lengths available.

Hand brush
For scrubbing hard-to-clean areas.

Cleaning Pool Equipment

The owner's manuals for your pump and filter outline whatever routine maintenance the machine requires. Inspect pumps and filters once a month, or whenever you notice the water getting dirty or sluggish.

A biological filter's media bed requires a light raking about once a month to remove accumulated debris. About twice a year, you'll need to either vacuum or backflush the system to get rid of excess sludge and sediments. A properly sized and maintained media bed will likely last several years. A pressurized sand filter needs frequent backwashing. The filter has a slide or rotary valve that controls the flow of water. If you must backwash your filter often and notice debris in the pool, open the filter and check the condition of the bed. If you find caked dirt in the sand it's time to replace the sand.

Cleaning pumps

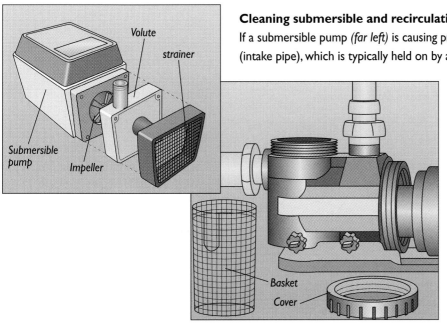

Volute
strainer
Submersible pump
Impeller
Basket
Cover

Cleaning submersible and recirculating pumps
If a submersible pump *(far left)* is causing problems, check the strainer and volute (intake pipe), which is typically held on by a few screws. Flush out the volute and the impeller with a strong jet of water, then reassemble the pump and test it to be sure it functions normally. If you have a surface, or recirculating, pump *(near left)*, you will need to clean debris from the strainer basket. To remove the basket, shut off the power; if the pump is below water level, turn off any valves. Then take off the cover, lift out the basket, and either clean it or replace it with a spare unit.

Cleaning cartridge filters

Hosing the filter clean
To clean a cartridge filter, simply remove the cartridge and hose it off, directing the water at an angle to the cartridge to remove the dirt. Return it to the housing, replace the cover, and seal it, then restart the system.

Water Chemistry

Water chemistry in a garden pool refers to the balancing of the several factors critical to water quality and the health of water plants and fish. Measure the pH, or potential hydrogen, of your pool water before introducing any plants or fish, and on a regular basis thereafter. The pH test will tell you where the water stands in terms of its acidity and alkalinity. On a logarithmic scale of 0 (total acidity) to 14 (total alkalinity), the ideal pH range for a garden pond is between 6.8 and 7.6.

Soda ash or sodium bicarbonate raises the pH; phosphoric acid, sodium bisulfate, or vinegar will lower it. Most of these products are available under simpler proprietary names. A test kit that shows acid and alkaline or digital pH testers will help you determine how much acid or alkali to add to the water. With some kits, you test the water by adding a reagent—a chemical substance—in liquid or tablet form to a precise amount of pool water contained in a device called a test block; comparing the resulting color variations with those shown on the test block tells what chemicals are needed. Other

WATER-TESTING ACCESSORIES

There are a variety of commercial pH and oxygen testers. Three of the most common ones are shown below. Consult a pond supplier for more information.

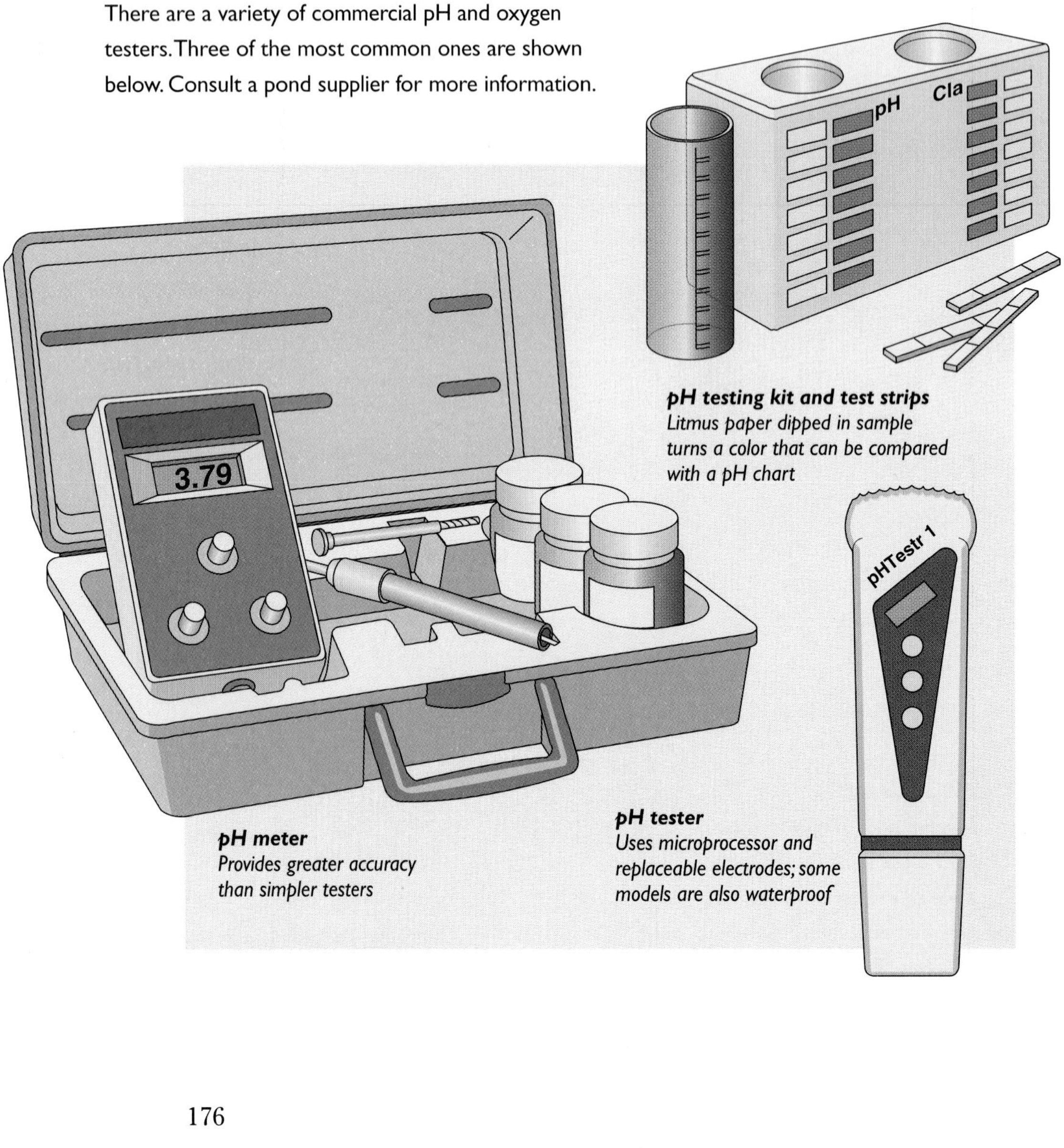

pH testing kit and test strips
Litmus paper dipped in sample turns a color that can be compared with a pH chart

pH tester
Uses microprocessor and replaceable electrodes; some models are also waterproof

pH meter
Provides greater accuracy than simpler testers

3.79

pHTestr 1

kits use paper strips that change color when dipped into the water. Again, the resulting hue is compared with a printed chart for interpretation. Test-kit reagents must be fresh; throw them away once they're more than 12 months old. Many modern testers, or pH meters, work digitally. In these models, an electrode is dipped in the water and provides a quick, extremely precise reading.

In addition to pH testing, you should test a fish pond for ammonia, nitrite, and oxygen levels, particularly if fish are dying. If none of these is out of balance, test the water hardness. Hardness testing kits should be available at aquarium and pond supply stores.

Concentrations of both ammonia and nitrites should be kept as low as possible. You can buy separate kits and devices to monitor these factors, or a multitest kit that will measure pH, ammonia, and nitrites.

To alter either ammonia or nitrites, small, gradual water changes are necessary until the substances come down to undetectable levels. The chart on page 178 will help you to identify common problems with water chemistry and their solutions.

Lastly, both chlorine and chloramines are toxic to fish. Chlorine will dissipate out of standing water in a few days, but you'll need to take chemical steps if your water supply has chloramines added to it. Proprietary chemicals are available for dealing with both chlorine and chloramines; even small amounts of water for "topping up" must be treated in problem areas.

One final danger to water quality is pollution. Beyond the fairly

While they are by no means a necessity for the water garden, ultraviolet sterilizers do provide fish pond owners with an added defense against waterborne algae as well as many bacteria, viruses, and fungi that may attack valuable koi. As water passes through a UV sterilizer, the unit produces light at specific wavelengths which work to kill germs, thereby reducing the number of microorganisms—including, most importantly, algae—in the water. Sterilizers are available in various strengths and in dozens of models. Consult a local pond supplier for a model suited to your pond.

Ultraviolet sterilizer

PARTIAL WATER CHANGES

One way to help ensure a healthy pond is by carrying out occasional partial water changes throughout the water gardening season. This involves more than simply topping up the pool as water evaporates in the heat of summer. Topping up is helpful, but as water evaporates, salts and waste materials become more concentrated in the water.

A partial change involves draining and replacing approximately 20 percent of the water in the pond, diluting these harmful concentrations and adding renewed vitality to the pond environment. Start by using a drain, pump, or siphon to remove

20 percent of the water. For the best possible effect, the water should be drained from near the bottom of the pond, where wastes are most heavily concentrated. You will probably have to clear leaves or other debris from the end of the hose from time to time.

When the correct amount is drained, fill the pond back to its normal level. Rainwater is the best choice for refilling, but it is unlikely you will have enough on hand. Tap water is fine, though once it is added, you should also add a commercial tap water conditioner following manufacturer's instructions.

common problems of rotting leaves and fish excrement, dangerous pollutants might include anything from pesticides and herbicides to oils and paints. If you think that pollution of one kind or other is causing problems in your pond, change part or all of the water. Then run all the water through a biological filter. Also keep in mind that the more the water is agitated, by a pump or moving water feature, the better toxic gases can escape the pond.

Lastly, when monitoring your water quality, bear in mind that the size of the pool will have an effect on the speed with which chemical imbalances overtake the pond. In smaller ponds, pH, oxygen, nitrite and ammonia levels can fluctuate rapidly. Monitor these indicators vigorously to prevent serious problems.

WATER DIAGNOSTIC CHART			
	LOW PH (ACID)	**HIGH PH (ALKALINE)**	**LACK OF OXYGEN**
Symptoms	Fish fins reddish in color. Fish prone to disease. Fish die inexplicably. Plants' growth stunted. Biological filters ineffective.	Fish prone to disease. Fish gills damaged. Plant growth stunted. Oxygenators covered in white film. Biological filters ineffective.	Water is darker than normal. Water has foul odor. Fish remain near pool surface. Larger fish die inexplicably.
Causes	Fish waste. Decomposing plants and vegetable matter. Soft (low in calcium) water in pond.	Lime leaking into pool. High algae content in water.	Excess fish food decomposing in water. Pump malfunctioning or not running. Pool overcrowded with fish. Too much of surface covered by plants. High algae content in water. Hot, humid weather.
Remedies	Add plants. Add commercial pond pH buffer following manufacturer's instructions. Carry out partial water change.	Stop feeding for two days. Coat lime surfaces with lime sealer. Make partial water change. Reduce algae content of pool. Add commercial pond pH buffer following manufacturer's instructions.	Reduce levels of algae. Remove some fish. Ensure pump is running; operate moving water features like waterfalls overnight. Carry out partial water change. Reduce percentage of pond surface covered with plants.

Pool Repairs

Flexible liners, fiberglass shells, and concrete may develop cracks or leaks due to an accident or just from gradual wear and tear. Here's how to attack the problems.

Liner and concrete repairs are shown starting below. To repair fiberglass, use a standard fiberglass repair kit, containing sections of fiberglass and a two-part epoxy adhesive consisting of resin and hardener. If serious cracks are evident, you have an improperly supported shell; drain the pool and check its structural support.

Repairing a liner pool

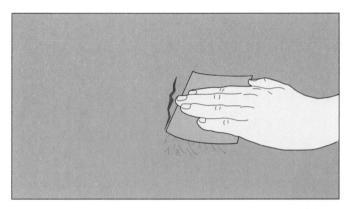

1 Preparing the liner
If you are repairing a PVC liner, apply PVC primer to the damaged area, then roughen the area with sandpaper *(left)*.

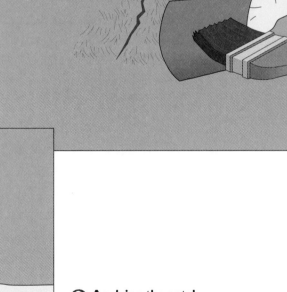

2 Preparing patch
Cut a liner patch to extend 6" on either side of the tear. Apply solvent cement to the liner and the patch with a paintbrush. Make sure the cement extends beyond the damaged area, while remaining within the edges of the patch.

3 Applying the patch
Set the patch in place by hand and smooth it in place *(left)*. If possible, use a pair of sandbags to weight the patch until the solvent dries.

Patching a crack in concrete

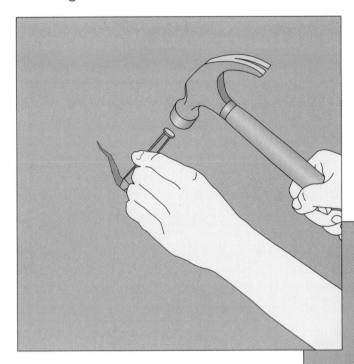

1 Widening the crack
With a cold chisel and a hammer, remove loose material and enlarge the crack, smoothing the edges as much as possible. Tap the chisel lightly, being careful not to gouge too deeply into the concrete *(left)*.

2 Preparing to fill the crack
Dip a paintbrush in water and wet the crack and surrounding area along its entire length. If bits of concrete come loose, remove them.

3 Applying patching compound
With a wooden float or a trowel, work patching compound into the crack until it is filled and the surface is even. Portland cement or hydraulic patching mixture containing portland cement are suitable for use. Follow the instructions provided by the manufacturer. Several quick-drying compounds are formulated for making repairs underwater. Repeat the procedure on all remaining cracks before proceeding to Step 4.

4 Etching the pool

Once all cracks are patched and while they are still damp, etch the concrete of the entire pool with muriatic acid, mixing one part acid and two parts tap water in a nonmetallic bucket. (Always add acid to water, not water to acid.) Wearing rubber gloves, protective goggles, and galoshes, apply the acid on all surfaces with a pool brush as shown above.

Pool Safety

Here are a few rules that will help provide a safe environment around the water garden.

• More than anyone, children are at risk around the water garden. Inform them of the danger and monitor them whenever they are around the pond. In addition, erect a rock wall around the pond, or design a wide, shallow edging of plants and either rocks or pebbles. A wire mesh placed over the pond or a clear glass or plastic table that sits in the water just under the surface are extreme measures to ensure no one falls in the water. For large ponds, the mesh just needs to extend around the edges of the water.

• When installing electrical controls, be sure they they are hidden from or out of reach of children.

• To prevent slipping, ensure all surfaces adjacent to the pond provide good traction.

• With large ponds, you will need to erect a fence around the water. Fit it with a childproof lock and ensure it is large enough to keep neighboring children out of the pond area.

• When designing the pool, make sure to provide a ledge or "step" to give anyone who does fall in an easy way to get out of the water.

5 Painting the pool

With a paint roller, apply two or three coats of paint or plastic cement sealer on the entire inside of the pool. To ensure the best possible result, follow the paint manufacturer's instructions carefully during this process.

Dealing with Plant Pests and Diseases

Pond plants tend to suffer fewer attacks from disease than their land-based cousins, but that does not mean they are problem free. Water lilies in particular are prone to cercosporiosis, a fungal disease that begins with spots on the leaves and, if left untreated, will render those leaves dead, stunting the growth of the entire plant. The most effective method of control is removing the infected leaves.

The water lily also happens to be a popular target of a common garden pest—the aphid. Control aphids by washing affected leaves. Heavier infestations can be handled by using an oil spray at growing-season strength; this will not have an adverse affect on fish, snails, or plants. Spray on cloudy days or in the evening to prevent leaf scorch.

Avoid using chemical treatments whenever possible. They are pollutants and can be very harmful to fish. BT *(Bacillus thuringiensis)* is one insecticide safe for use near pools and is effective for combating caterpillars, slugs, and other pests that feed on marginal plants. (A variety of BT is designed for eradicating mosquitoes, and should pose no problem to fish.) If you are worried about its effect on pets, try using one of the many natural methods. Here are two options: 1. Bury a soda bottle, one quarter full of water, so its spout is at ground level. Pests will investigate, fall into the bottle, and drown. 2. Cut a grapefruit in half and set one half peel-side-up beside the pond. Slugs and other pests will crawl beneath it to feed. Once a day or so, lift it and remove the pests.

In general, fish are the best controllers of pests, devouring them or eating their eggs.

Use the chart below as a rough guide for treating affected plants. If difficulties persist, consult a botanist or watergardening expert.

PLANT PESTS AND DISEASES

PEST OR DISEASE	VICTIMS	SYMPTOMS	REMEDIES
Aphid	Aquatic plants, especially water lilies.	Small white bugs on leaves or leaves that have been eaten.	Pick them off by hand; wash leaves with hose.
China mark moth	Aquatic plants, especially water lilies.	Small oval holes in leaves; larvae clusters near leaf edges.	Remove moths from pond using small fish net; pick all caterpillars off leaves. Remove leaves with eggs.
Snail	All aquatic plants.	Plants that have been eaten; stunted growth.	Remove snails by hand; use water-garden-safe insecticide such as BT.
Water-lily beetle	Water lilies.	Leaves that have been eaten.	Fish, particularly goldfish, will eat them.
Leaf-mining midge	All aquatic plants.	Leaves than have been eaten; sometimes skeletonized.	Remove infested leaves.
Fungal infections	Water lilies and certain marginals (Most frequently *Caltha* spp.).	Lilies: Black spots on leaves; leaves that are black and dry around edges. Marginals: Mildew on leaves.	Lilies: Cut off affected leaves; remove plant from pool and apply fungicide to remaining affected leaves. Marginals: Cut off affected leaves; remove plant from pool and treat with fungicide.
Lily crown rot	Water lilies, particularly those that have been moved or recently planted.	Leaves become yellow; black spots start at leaf center and expand; crown is rotted.	Remove plants from pool and destroy.

Preparing Plants for Winter

To help ensure the health of plant life in the pond, and to save the cost of replacing plants at the start of each new season, it's worth spending some time before winter doing a little preparation. This is particularly true if you live in a colder climate where there is a risk of the pond freezing.

Hardy water lilies do not require any special care. They will prepare themselves naturally and reappear the next spring. Tropical varieties are a different matter. Cut off the tubers—the walnut-sized growths at the crown of the plant—and store them in containers in a dark room over the winter. In the spring, place the tubers in a pot and return them to the water garden.

Floaters normally require little care. They generally die down into winter buds which fall to the bottom of the pool and come to life in spring. But to be sure of their return, collect several of the winter buds and store them in containers filled with water with a small amount of soil at the bottom. Provide them with good light over the winter and they will start up early in the spring and can be added to the pool.

Generally, moisture-loving plants and marginals and should be cut back to remove all dead or dying leaves before winter. Most plants in baskets should then be lowered but not submerged in deeper water in the pool. Others are best brought in, so their bulbs or root systems can be stored in a container inside. Consult with a botanist or a water gardening expert if you are in doubt about a given species.

Trimming and storing plants

Cutting back marginals
Using a pair of long-handled pruning shears, cut back marginals like cattails to about one third of their height. As an added precaution, you can cover the plants with a layer of straw.

Storing marginals indoors
Marginals in baskets can be brought inside to ensure their survival over the winter. Cut them back to one third their full height (*right*), removing all dead growth, then store them in a dry, dark spot in your home.

Fish Diseases

As with humans, fish can be adversely affected by stress, which can give rise to a range of diseases. Stressful conditions include overcrowding, rough handling and transport, insufficient oxygen, temperature swings, and toxins in the water. If your pool is maintained properly, you should have little trouble—especially after the fish have been in the pool for a while—but make it a habit to observe your fish on a regular basis to check for potential problems.

Fish diseases are the result of either parasites, bacteria, or a fungus. To help you identify the problem, see the chart below.

Mail-order sources and pet stores sell many brand name medications for treating fish diseases. Standard treatments for parasites included trichlorfon, and a mixture of malachite green and formalin. A variety of wide-spectrum antibiotics treat bacteria and fungi. A salt bath often can help clear up many fish diseases. Mix in rock salt at the rate of 44 pounds per 1,000 gallons of pool water; or isolate the affected fish and treat it for one hour at twice that concentration. A salt bath is a one-time proposition: salt concentrations build up in the water until flushed out.

Consult a veterinarian, koi expert, koi club, or textbook for help with any problem you don't understand. If you have a biological filter, be sure that whatever treatment you choose will not affect the bacteria in your filter media.

FISH DISEASE REFERENCE CHART	
DISEASE	**SYMPTOMS**
Anchor worm Parasite	Tiny twiglike worms, up to $1/2$" in length, attach themselves to skin; twin egg sacs may be visible at end.
Cloudy eye Nonspecific	As the name indicates, symptom is milky cloud over eyes; fish loses energy, appetite.
Columnarius (mouth fungus) Nonspecific	Actually a bacteria, not a fungus. Usually attacks head and mouth region. Contagious to other fish.
Dropsy (pinecone disease) Bacteria	Scales stand out from body as on a pinecone, hence the name. Swollen abdomen is common. Usually fatal.
Finrot/Tailrot Bacteria	Begins with light, foggy patches; progresses to bloody and rotted tail or fins. Indicative of unclean pond conditions.
Fish lice Parasite	Twin suckers attach to skin; lice are light green or brown, up to $1/2$" in diameter, hard to see unaided; fish rub against pool sides and rocks in effort to "brush off" lice.
Flukes (gill or skin) Parasite	Fish swim with jerky motion, mouth at surface as if exhausted (if gill flukes). Fish skin appears whitish; fish attempt to rub against objects in pond (if skin flukes).
Fungus Fungus	Cotton- or wool-like appearance on body or fins. Attacks previously injured or stressed fish. May appear whitish or even greenish (mixed with algae).
Ich (white spot) Parasite	White spots may cover body; on close observation, "noodlelike" parasites may be visible. Fish rub against objects.
Leeches Parasite	Flattened worms, up to 1 inch long, brown or greyish in color.
Oxygen depletion Water condition	Fish mouth at surface, appear exhausted.
Ulcer (hole-in-the-side disease) Nonspecific	Ulcer appears on fish body; often fatal.

Helping Fish Cope with Winter

Depending on the climate of your region, you can vary the depth of your pond to keep it from freezing. A pump will also serve to prevent freeze-up. Lack of oxygen can be a problem, though; you may wish to run a small pool heater that keeps a hole open to allow some air exchange. An improvised pool cover—netting and straw, canvas

awning material, plastic grid and opaque sheeting or more formal glazing—can help maintain the water temperature. But your best choice is still a small pool heater. If ice cover does form, never break through by banging as this can end up killing your fish. Instead, use a pot of boiling water to melt a section of ice.

If you have a small tub garden with just a few goldfish, simply move them inside to warmer quarters. If you have a large pond, but are uncomfortable leaving valuable fish there over the winter, set up an indoor aquarium and keep the fish inside until the spring. Two methods of providing an oxygen hole in a pond are shown below.

Maintaining open water in winter

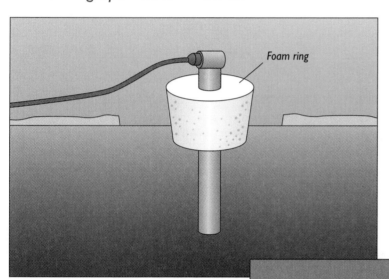

Foam ring

Using a pond heater
Many suppliers carry electric pond heaters, which will keep a small area of water open in even the coldest weather. These are typically brass rods connected to an electrical supply and kept afloat by a foam ring like the model shown at left.

Opening a hole in ice
If you are unable to use a pool heater to maintain open water, use a pot of boiling water as shown at right. Simply boil the water, then set the pot on the ice and allow a few minutes for it to melt.

Supplies and More Information

Whether you already have your garden installed, or you are still in the planning stages, the listing below will prove invaluable. The suppliers listed below can supply you with everything from flexible liners and fiberglass shells to submersible pumps and oxygenating plants. Some mail-order sources even send goldfish and koi—by express mail only, of course. This is only a partial listing, including a sampling of large, national mail-order sources. Smaller, more regional companies, plus those specializing in water plants or koi, abound. Garden pool enthusiasts and builders can also steer you to local favorites.

The short sampling of clubs and associations will also prove useful. They should be able to provide you with information you need, or point you to a local club or supplier that can. In addition, they will be able to put you in touch with other water gardeners with whom you can exchange information.

SUPPLIERS

Aquasculpture
200 Thompson Blvd.
Ville St. Laurent, Quebec
Canada H4N 1B9

Aquatic Eco-Systems, Inc.
1767 Benbow Court
Apopka, FL 32703

Flotec
P.O. Box 342
Delevan, WI 53115

Hermitage Garden Pools
P.O. Box 3561
Canastota, NY 13032

Kingkoi International
5879 Avis Lane
Harrisburg, PA 17112

Lilypons Water Gardens
P.O. Box 10
Lilypons, MD 21717

Maryland Aquatic Nurseries, Inc.
3427 North Furnace Rd.
Jarrettsville, MD 21084

McAllister Water Gardens
7420 St. Helena Highway
Yountville, CA 94599

Moore Water Gardens
P.O. Box 70
Port Stanley, Ontario
Canada N5L 1J4

Paradise Water Gardens
14 May St.
Whitman, MA 02382

S. Scherer and Sons
104 Waterside Ave.
Northport, NY 11768

Serenity Ponds and Streams
4488 Candleberry Ave.
Seal Beach, CA 90740

Slocum Water Gardens
1101 Cypress Gardens Blvd.
Winter Haven, FL 33880

Tetra Pond
3001 Commerce St.
Blacksburg, VA 24060

Van Ness Water Gardens
2460 N. Euclid Ave.
Upland, CA 91786

Water Creations
2507 East 21st St.
Des Moines, IA 50317

Waterford Gardens
74 East Allendale Rd.
Saddle River, NJ 07458

Wicklein's Aquatic Farm & Nursery, Inc.
1820 Cromwell Bridge Rd.
Baltimore, MD 21234

CLUBS AND ASSOCIATIONS

American Society of Landscape Architects
4401 Connecticut Ave., N.W.
Fifth Floor,
Washington, DC 20008

Associated Koi Clubs of America
P.O. Box 1
Midway City, CA 92655

Capital Area Pond & Water Garden Society
P.O. Box 66424
Baton Rouge, LA 70896

Delaware Valley Water Garden Society
1736 Green Valley Rd.
Havertown, PA 19083

International Water Lily Society
P.O. Box 2309
Columbia, MD 21045

Mid-Atlantic Koi Club
185 Kingfisher Dr.
Middletown, NJ 07748

National Pond Society
286 Village Parkway
Marietta, GA 30067

National Spa and Pool Institute
2111 Eisenhower Ave.
Alexandria, VA 22314

Washington Koi and Water Garden Society
10021 Evergreen Way
Everett, WA 96204

Index

187

Acknowledgments

The editors wish to thank the following:

American Fisheries Society, Bethesda, MD

Aquasculpture, St. Laurent, Que.

Aquatic Eco-Systems, Inc., Apopka, FL

Association of Professional Landscape Designers, Chicago, IL

Biodôme de Montréal, Montreal, Que.

Joel Burkard, Bothell, WA

City of Stockton Permit Center, Stockton, CA

Cyprio Limited, Peterborough, UK

Downes Pool, Wheeling, IL

Earth Images Foundation, St. Catharines, Ont.

Ecomuseum, Ste. Anne de Bellevue, Que.

Emperor Aquatics, Pottstown, PA

Garden Concepts, Inc., Glenview, IL

Hermitage Gardens, Canastota, NY

Jacuzzi, Inc., Little Rock, AR

Linda Jarosiewicz, Montreal, Que.

Little Giant Pump Company, Oklahoma City, OK

Macon Bureau of Inspection and Fees, Macon, GA

Maryland Aquatic Nurseries, Jarrettsville, MD

Montreal Botanical Garden/Jardin botanique de Montréal, Montreal, Que.

Joseph E. Morris, Fisheries/Aquaculture Extension Specialist, Department of
    Animal Ecology, Iowa State University, Ames, IA

Multi-Duti Manufacturing Inc., Beaverton, OR

Pan Intercorp, Bothell, WA

Portland Cement Association, Skokie, IL

Potomac Waterworks, Oakland, CA

Royal Ontario Museum, Centre for Biodiversity and Conservation Biology,
    Toronto, Ont.

Tetra Pond, Blacksburg, VA

Wardley Corporation, Secaucus, NJ

Water Creations, Des Moines, IL

The following people also assisted in the preparation of this book:
Jean-Pierre Bourgeois, Lorraine Doré, Joan Beth Erickson, Normand Fleury,
Gabriel Gauthier, Pascale Hueber, Mathieu Raymond-Beaubien, Raymond
Saumure, Britta Swartz

Picture Credits